Dry Bones Live

Also by Robert C. Worley

A Gathering of Strangers: Understanding the Life of Your Church
Revised and updated

Dry Bones Live

Helping Congregations Discover New Life

Robert H. Craig
Robert C. Worley

Westminster/John Knox Press
Louisville, Kentucky

This book is a complete revision of *Dry Bones, Breathe*, copyright © 1978 The Center for the Study of Church Organizational Behavior of McCormick Theological Seminary (Chicago, 1978).

Scripture quotations from the New Revised Standard Version of the Bible are copyright © 1989 by the Division of Christian Education of the National Council of the Churches of Christ in the U.S.A., and are used by permission.

Book design by Peggy Claire Calhoun

First edition

Published by Westminster/John Knox Press
Louisville, Kentucky

This book is printed on acid-free paper that meets the American National Standards Institute Z39.48 standard. ∞

PRINTED IN THE UNITED STATES OF AMERICA
9 8 7 6 5 4 3 2 1

Library of Congress Cataloging-in-Publication Data

Craig, Robert H. (Robert Hugh), 1946–
   Dry bones live : helping congregations discover new life / Robert H. Craig, Robert C. Worley. — 1st ed.
      p.   cm.
   Rev. ed. of: Dry bones, breathe / Robert C. Worley. c 1978.
   Includes bibliographical references and index.
   ISBN 0-664-25316-4 (alk. paper)

   1.Church renewal—United States. 2. United States—Church history—20th century. I. Worley, Robert C. II. Worley, Robert C. Dry bones, breathe. III. Title.
BV600.2.C68 1992
262'.001'7—dc20   92-28535

*To those pastors, church leaders, and members of
churches from whom we have learned.*

Contents

List of Illustrations

Preface

The churches that have historically been referred to as "mainline" are currently seen by some as being on the "sideline"—antiquated, representing the values of elites who have become unresponsive to the needs of people in contemporary culture. Much attention is currently given to this perceived phenomenon in articles, books, and lectures. Some of the criticism is undoubtedly true, but these churches, as with all Christian churches, can be activated and mobilized for profound Christian ministry.

This book focuses on the church as a living people who exist as a worshiping, praying, reflective, spiritual entity within which diverse Christian commitments and loyalty to different Christian traditions exist. On the other hand, the church lives as a complex organization that sometimes maintains corporate behavior that has been outgrown by its commitments and loyalties. Has the mainline church outgrown some of its old ways of doing things without providing for dynamic values, loyalties, and commitments to be expressed? Is it possible that doing the same things in a changing environment is not really doing the same things? Might organizational patterns wisely designed to pursue current mission be transformed to facilitate new ends? We believe in positive responses to these questions and have written a book aimed at the revitalization of church organizations, especially ones which perceive themselves to be the victims of outside forces. We believe that wise, public, and beneficent processes can be implemented which will enable groups of faithful people more fully to understand and empower mission within the environment that God has provided them.

The first edition of this book, *Dry Bones, Breathe* (Chicago: Center for the Study of Church Organizational Behavior of McCormick Theological Seminary, 1978), has been rewritten, reordered, and updated with new material. Additional chapters have been provided on vision and commitment. A new bibliographical essay is provided to point the reader to additional sources in the theory and practice of revitalizing congregations.

We are grateful to McCormick Theological Seminary for its support of our research and reflection. The seminary's Board of Trustees, its president,

David Ramage, and our colleagues have all been generous with encouragement and resources. Many of the seminary's Doctor of Ministry groups have provided us an arena for teaching and student-led research. Many of these groups have tested, refined, and contributed to the theories behind this work. Carol Gorsky, our writing consultant, and Lynne Schweppe and Doran Hill, our typists, deserve great praise for their careful and helpful contributions.

Our greatest thanksgiving is reserved for our families, who have permitted and encouraged long hours of hard work to proceed around, away from, and among them. Their love truly inspires.

Introduction

Most members of congregations are passive. A small minority do the maintenance work of congregational life. Fewer still are involved in caring for members and the community. The major amount of time, energy, and money comes from fewer than 15 percent of the membership in most congregations. Increasingly, attendance of 20 to 30 percent of the members at worship is viewed as acceptably normal. When members do attend worship, they are passive, except in those rare congregations that have searched for an understanding of what it means to be a worshiping people, rather than an audience at a performance of the preacher, organist, and choir. Annual meetings where fewer than 10 percent of the members make decisions for the congregation are vivid evidence of passivity. The minister and a few laity are the principal actors in most congregations. This has been the dominant pattern for several centuries.

This pattern seems problematic when viewed through Søren Kierkegaard's metaphor of "the theater of worship." Kierkegaard sees the worshipers as actors in relationship to God, who is the audience. To attain this reversal of typical roles, faithful leadership requires new theory and practice.

With some few notable exceptions, members have been loyal, obedient, fearful, and passive. Clergy and the lay elite of the society and the church have acted too frequently to keep members passive. Books of discipline, church order, and manuals of operation offer adequate testimony to the ability of ministers and leaders to establish rights for themselves, but none for congregations. Claims of "divine office" and "divine rights" have covered many sins of clergy and lay leaders. Charismatic preaching of clergy, appeal to loyalty, and systems of authority have all been used to maintain a compliant laity.

In many congregations, the standing of an active church member is defined in terms of frequency of church attendance, contribution of money, and engagement in maintenance work.

In this book an active church member is defined as one who is living out Christian faith commitments. If church members are to live this way, then ministers and congregational leaders need a theory and style of leadership that will challenge and equip members to become active, since past patterns of leadership and membership have kept members passive. Equally important, leaders need a new understanding of the church, or perhaps, more accurately, they need an understanding that is more fully informed by scripture and contemporary theology, which insists that the church is a covenant people called by God to be actors in their faith community and in the world.

The last four decades have been years of resurgence in biblical study. This study of both Old and New Testaments has pointed to an active, corporate people. It stands dramatically opposed to the minister-centered, passive, individualistic nature of church membership. Constructive theology insists that scripture informs us of God who is *for us and for the world*, not just for me as solitary individual, and that we are for God as we are for God's world. Contemporary theology describes the church as people who are actively living out their commitments as they care for each other. Images of the church found in contemporary writings confirm the active character of God's people as reconciling agents, community of faith, community of moral discourse, people of God, covenanting people, and servant people. These active images imply a style of leadership that will seek to guide, inform, and assist a membership in assessing the coherence between the images and the life of the people. This means that a community thinks and reflects about the character and quality of their life. Leaders do not do it for them.

Members are responsible and accountable for the quality of their membership. Discipline, loyalty, and fear of authority are not sufficient to maintain a quality of life in a culture that has experienced various liberation movements, political parties, community organizations, voluntary associations, and consumer and other issue-oriented groups. Actually, the culture of many mainline churches challenges persons to actively live out commitments and provides leadership and processes to help people to so live. Church leadership frequently exhorts people to activity, but does not have a facilitating style or set of processes to help members live out commitments as the church.

In order for a Christianized culture to flourish, leaders must offer both moral vision and moral processes that encourage the public good. This envisioning is a practice of leadership that guides the church into God's desirable future. Leaders must gaze wisely into the future and then guide others into a God-given vision. Too much organizational leadership theory lacks this foundational theological understanding and thus begins with finite human reflections limited to the status quo.

Christianized culture is also reinforced through moral processes. The means and the ends of mission must be in moral concert. Thinking, dreaming, inquiring, planning, choosing, implementing, and evaluating must be accomplished in visible ways in which members of the body may participate. Participation in the life of the community of faith is not something to be accomplished vicariously by elites on behalf of others. Organizationally, no less than spiritually, each believer possesses the right of participation in the Body of Christ. Faithful people have the right to engage in good and benevolent processes, which actively draw them together to carry on their God-given mission.

People possess normative values, full of meaning, which they endeavor to pursue in their own lives and within their communities. We have acknowledged that too few leaders guide communities in envisioning a future full of those values. Neither do enough leaders equip communities to develop processes that bring about actual movement in concert with the visions. The motivating interest in doing theology is the concern for such transformation and not just for rationality. Certainly values must be assessed in order to facilitate appropriate change, but assessment alone does not accomplish change. Transformational change theory does not merely collect and analyze data, it also develops vision out of clear values in order that activity may be designed to live into that vision. Values are applied to understanding, through participatory processes, in order that constructive change may result. Such activity is not merely rational but mobilizing, full of mandates that require accountability.

There are many current efforts to understand, interpret, and express Christian faith that offer insights about the theological import of faithful Christians and Christian communities as actors within history. In their transformations, the faithful and the church become sources of theological truth and understanding. New faith can and does spring from a new practice of faithfulness. People become shapers of the future through active participation within the lives of their communities. The challenge for church leadership is to continue to discover structures and processes that will lead all people into such helpful change.

This book is for leaders who desire to create the conditions under which an active, whole people will form, as contrasted with leaders who are satisfied with a passive collection of individuals. This is a book with a theology that includes a theory and practice about people formation, people nurture, and people maintenance. The focus—to which we now turn—makes this theory and practice distinct from earlier theories of renewal.

Part I

The Puzzle

1

Options for Renewing the Church

Since the late 1940s, numerous strategies have been developed for renewing congregations. Characteristic of all have been their attempts to develop a theology for the church that would make sense out of faith and life. The uniqueness of each strategy has been found in its educational resources and in its design or plan. Numerous study books, pamphlets, and audio-visuals for the implementation of each strategy have been developed, and pastors and leadership groups have gathered together interested individuals to study these materials. It has been assumed that the participants would be the nucleus of new congregational vitality and in many instances the assumption was valid. Many adults with a very poor or limited background in the church school and in the church have been helped enormously with their personal questions about Christian faith and life through one or more of these strategies. However, the overall effect on congregational life has been limited, except when a significant number within the congregation—a critical mass—have caught fire and altered the spirit, character, and direction of the congregation.

The more general result has been that adults with new personal insights, but still without access to organizational mechanisms that could implement them, have become apathetic and alienated from the traditional leadership of their congregations. The path from new insights about Christian faith to expression in congregational life has never been clear in any of these strategies. Consequently, individuals and groups who have gained new insights about faith and life—yet sensed that they have been deprived of meaningful institutional ways to express them—have organized against those whom they perceive as depriving them. Rump groups, cadres, and increasing political activity have frequently been outlets for such perceptions and energy. Ministers and governing boards across every denomination have felt the tension and frustration of such newly mobilized people, without realizing that the very strategies to which they had looked for help were bringing about the situation.

In this chapter the strengths of various types of church renewal strategies are described—along with their weaknesses. Then other holistic approaches to congregational renewal that takes seriously the integrated nature of congregational life, goals, and leadership are presented.

Renewal Groups and Centers

One popular set of strategies for congregational renewal has depended on teams of "experts" trained at renewal centers and sent into local churches to "share" renewal with congregational members. These strategies—almost invariably accompanying the development of new theological content—have focused on the home and family in an attempt to deepen the faith of all members, or they have concentrated on small groups that could be organized and mobilized to take over congregational leadership. The centers of renewal, which have generally had their own unique design for the future, have existed to draw people from congregations, give them a new theological content, and send them back to the congregation as a political cadre with revolutionary intentions, as a group mobilized and committed to particular social and ethical issues, or as a group working to bring personnel from the centers of renewal to share their content and style with others. The assumption has been that these people would mobilize others so that a critical mass within a congregation might be developed to alter the congregation's style and direction. Many contemporary forms of evangelism have been built around this strategy, with such descriptive titles as "lay renewal," "lay witness," and "faith at work." The small group has been the mediating instrument between renewers and the congregation. The renewers have assumed that, if a sufficient number of small groups adopt the new content and style, new congregational life will develop. However, this dependence on outside specialists or technicians has frequently produced tension and divisiveness; the content and style of the external people, rather than congregational vitality, have become the major issue.

Preaching Renewal

The all-time favorite strategy of renewing congregational life has been to employ a "charismatic" preacher, one who can inspire and mobilize masses. Some of these preachers have found a receptive congregation and have been somewhat effective; others who have desired more vital congregations have preached with little or no avail. Meanwhile both the laity—and even seminary educational theories—frequently continue to place the burden for renewal on pastoral functions, particularly preaching. Clergy are educated to perform effectively in specialized functions: preaching, leading the liturgy, teaching, and counseling, with the all too frequent hidden assumption behind their education that preaching and calling are their most important activities. Yet many decent preachers and extensive callers have travelled the familiar path to the regional mental health service for ministers. Others live in situations like powder kegs ready to blow up, where only civility and lack of courage restrain members from openly expressing their frustrations. The most common situation is one in which clergy are frustrated because nothing happens in the congregation, even though they preach and call.

This failure of preaching has led to skepticism about its effectiveness on the one hand, or to the preacher's resignation from the ministry with a sense of failure on the other. There is a soberness and new inquiry about the role and effectiveness of preaching in strategies of revitalizing congregations. Many thoughtful clergy have begun to ask: How does the content of preaching lead to the transformation of congregational life? Does increased church attendance mean a more vital Christian congregation? How can the result of personal faith and commitment find expression in institutional church life? What are the processes by which individuals hear the gospel and work out its meaning, not only in personal terms, but also in its social and institutional implications? Is something more needed to supplement preaching in order to make faith effective and meaningful in institutional life? What conditions need to exist in a congregation so that persons hear and respond to preaching?

An impossible burden is placed on clergy when laity expect them to revitalize a whole institution—which includes the congregation with its history, culture, and patterns of thinking and behaving—through preaching alone.

Preaching is an extremely important part of developing vital congregations, but as a strategy of renewal it is only one of the institutional activities important for the transformation of congregational life and for the expression of Christian faith. Clergy cannot be employed to revitalize a congregation. They can only be instrumental in assisting the congregation to develop its own vitality.

After all, moral reflection and encouragement of individuals do not necessarily lead to corporate reflection and congregational action. There is no evidence to suggest that, by simply increasing the number of individuals who think morally in their personal lives, a person can produce moral institutions that genuinely express Christian faith in structure, political process, use of power, or goal setting. Moral and theologically sophisticated people do not necessarily apply their knowledge and commitments to congregational life, or to any other sphere of life. Most people interpret Christian faith in personal rather than social and institutional terms. Even when the preacher exhorts members to institutional action little happens, because institutions—such as congregations—are different from individuals, groups, and families. To transform congregational life requires knowledge, skill, and commitment.

Renewal Through Liturgy

The renewal of liturgy has been a third major strategy of church renewal. Some have assumed that through the reestablishment of traditional liturgy or the modified forms of liturgy, new vitality would come to congregations. The major problem here is that only part of the congregation participates in worship. Indeed, worshippers rarely constitute more than 40 to 50 percent of the membership. Further, the part of the congregation that does worship together is not of a single mind about liturgy. Contemporary forms appeal to one segment, while nineteenth century hymns, prayers, and responses are preferred by others. Alteration of liturgical forms increases the motivation and commitment of some members and alienates others. Experience working with congregations has revealed that much of the conflict has been due to disparate goals for congregational worship. Renewal often focuses on only one aspect of a congregation's life and leads to only modest gains, at best, in vitality. Some claim that effective preaching, as one aspect of liturgy, is more important in congregational activation than any other. Few congregations have participated in congregational processes developed for understanding their worship life and transforming that life into a vital and central part of living. It remains an activity primarily related to the pastor's performance, not the congregation's participation in worshiping God.

Educational Programs

Education is a joy and can be a worthwhile end in itself. It is, however, not a particularly good renewal methodology if detached from processes of commitment making and implementation. Too frequently church groups had hoped that renewal would happen if members were led to understand better key thoughts and issues through various forms and levels of Christian education. While such a move is essential in healthy renewal processes, the taking of this individualistic, rational step alone may prove problematic for participants. To understand incompletely and in isolation from others is frustrating. Education is to be highly valued, but not as a renewal strategy in itself.

Church Growth Movements

The renewal of the church as a result of commitments to Christ by a large number of its members is much discussed. Certainly the efforts directed toward growth are important for the life of the whole church. However, this particular renewal method is limited in its methodology. Much of the theory of church growth revolves around homogeneity. This theory asserts that people will be attracted to—and most quickly assimilated into—a community of believers whom they perceive to be similar to themselves. It is hard to imagine such a call to uniformity at the core of the gospel. In addition, there is a strategic limit to the usefulness of this method that makes it an impractical, if not unfaithful, churchwide methodology for renewal.

The church-growth methodology succeeds only where the resources are present to produce results. A pool of potential members who value homogeneity, and possess youthlike energy, time, money, and/or trust are needed. This methodology will therefore only work well for renewal in some environments. It will not be a helpful technique where the church community is depressed or lacks a pool of existing or potential members full of the kinds of gifts just identified. Church growth theory is environmentally bound to succeed only in limited contexts. Unfortunately, some congregational leaders cause themselves—or are caused by others—to judge the values and importance of valid ministries by the norms of this kind of church growth movement. To be limited in one environment by the gifts which God has given to others in another context is unjust and debilitating.

The leadership styles and ecclesiologies of some brands of church growth fall into leader-bound, passive membership patterns typical of too many congregations. The threat is that huge, passive congregations—full of persons uncommitted to or uninvolved with the gospel beyond their personal affirmation of faith—will be formed.

Renewal Through Mission Strategies

During the 1960s, numerous strategies of congregational renewal developed around the concept of mission. Race, urbanization, peace, technology, urban renewal, education in the city, political corruption, and community organization issues mobilized small groups of members in many congregations. A particular issue was the central feature of this renewal strategy. However, in most congregations, the leadership were often successful at sealing off a large portion of the congregation from the influence, concern, and commitment of these small groups. The resources of few congregations were activated to focus effectively on any particular issue. Consequently, the problems needing resolution persisted while the members, with their energy and commitment dissipated, became apathetic, disillusioned, and hostile—or switched their allegiance to the next emerging issue. Effective response to issues takes institutional commitment and resources. Small groups of issue-oriented people were generally ineffective and frequently alienated the needed institutional resources. The focus on the issue was so intense and consumed so much energy that no attention was given to building support and mobilizing the congregation, or to minimizing resistance and opposition. Because there was little coalition building around an issue, many advocates were perceived as intolerant, arrogant, or doctrinaire, unable to see the broader needs of congregational life. This polarization around issues rendered many congregations weak and ineffective, unable to care effectively for either self or community.

Most attempts at congregational renewal through focusing on community issues have been markedly ineffective. A few congregations, primarily in rapidly changing urban neighborhoods, have been able to mobilize their members by focusing on problems in the surrounding community. But even these few congregations have experienced dramatic shifts in membership. Large congregations have become small, made up of a faithful remnant and new residents in the community with similar commitments.

Renewal Through Social Policy Formation

The church has an important prophetic calling that commands forceful and public comment on urgent societal issues. When the church does speak publicly in such ways, negative individual reactions may follow, which vary from claims that it is out of its field of expertise, to views that it should not be concerned with such things, to feelings of disenfranchisement by members who do not feel represented. It is the last of these responses that reveals the limits of societal policy formation as a renewal methodology.

As important as social policy formation and presentation is for church bodies as parts of their ministries, this methodology frequently limits renewal as much as it stimulates. When church members sense that they are being committed by others to positions around which they have no awareness or with which they disagree, they frequently react negatively. Such reactions often undermine the very kinds of implementation the policy is meant to empower. Church members are unlikely to work to bring about ends that are unclear or problematic for them, merely because a presumably authoritative church body makes a prophetic claim. To be sure, the church is called to take a prophetic stance and be God's principality in a world of principalities, but, to be equally sure, isolated social policies and statements are greatly limited as processes of renewal within the church.

Renewal Through Sensitivity Training

The focus on the world outside the congregation in the 1960s was followed by an inward focus in the early 1970s. Sensitivity training, T-groups, group therapy and counseling in the church, individual and group growth, human potential, and personal awareness all pointed to the new emphasis on self and the relation of self to others in congregational and secular life. The human potential movement successfully infiltrated many congregations, bringing with it a heightened awareness of self and others. Many trainers and devotees of the movement heralded the skills and insights from this movement as the essence of congregational renewal. Intimacy among members developed as a fundamental value and criterion for evaluating church membership. Frequently this was called spiritual renewal and was equated with intimacy.

However, the focus on individual and group growth and on team building simply was not adequate to deal with the complexity of goals, personal commitments, history, and culture found in congregations. Individual and group strategies cannot appropriately deal with the purposes, nature, ministry, and mission of congregations in turbulent environments. Some tools from this movement are valuable because they help people understand and relate more effectively to what is happening to other persons and groups. However, personal and group change do not necessarily bring about institutional change.

Renewal Through Organizational Development

Organizational development, or parish development—an offspring of the human relations movement—is another recently developed strategy of congregational renewal. It builds on the theory that the organization is people and assumes that those who matter most in parish life are leaders and leadership groups. Top management is the primary target, and training similar to the type found in many industries with organizational development staffs is prescribed. This strategy moves from leaders to problem solving, to conflict management, and to goal setting by leaders for the congregation.

Yet in a real sense leaders are the product of a congregation. Too much power and influence are usually attributed to leaders and leadership groups in the church, for leaders are influenced by the state of the congregation as much as they influence it. Goalless congregations tend to select goalless leaders. Furthermore, leadership groups without a mandate for performance and direction hesitate to step out beyond their perceived boundaries. Few leadership groups take risks when there is minimal or unknown support for their projects. Any renewal strategy that is targeted at leaders without a concurrent concern for the congregation as a whole can easily lead to frustration and paralysis.

Spiritual Renewal

Spiritual renewal is currently one of the most demanded and most needed emphases of the church. In Protestant groups a quest for deeper spiritual understanding, life, and expression is common today. Some of the faithful feel that in past reformations much of the church lost the best of the rich spiritual heritage of Roman Catholicism and Orthodox Christianity.

A concern about spiritual nurture is appropriate if the formation and nurture of individuals is perceived as a means of renewing the corporate church. A spiritual renewal method can include many of the weaknesses of other methods whereby individual growth is expected to accomplish corporate results. There are, however, appropriate means by which spiritual formation may be a function of the whole church body. This concept of faithful corporate spirituality proposes that in the upbuilding of the whole body and its life in the world, we are engaging in a spiritual matter. We are not to dismiss spiritual concerns but must address them more fully and deeply. Such a spiritual quest is at the heart of church renewal, and it is not for any of us alone. It is a quest in which the entire body of Christ is meant to function together in growthful ways. It is upon this spiritual journey that the remainder of this book embarks.

From this brief and admittedly limited description of dominant strategies of church renewal, it can be seen that most of these plans do not focus on the congregation itself. Parish development strategies based upon human relations theory of organizations with its emphasis on leadership and leadership groups, human relations training, and group growth ignore major aspects of congregational life. Renewal of congregational life requires transforming how church people live as congregations as well as how they speak and believe personally and relate to one another in groups. Most renewal efforts have not foundered upon "belief" or interpersonal relations, but upon lack of clarity of purpose and direction; the inability to modify structures, polity (the rules and procedures of doing business) and political processes; and the failure to deal adequately with issues of power. But the renewal of a congregation involves more than altering one aspect of congregational life; this is only the first step to renewal. The partial transformation may or may not be of consequence in taking the next steps. Transforming the whole is not the same as transforming a part. New liturgies, improved preaching, contemporary confessions of faith, modern studies of basic Christian beliefs, emphases on the community, human relations and organizational training for leaders—all these focus on only part of a congregation's life. Terrific struggles among various parts have led to paralysis in many church communities. This book recognizes and appreciates the contributions of the earlier renewal strategists, as will be evident in later chapters. The attempt here, however, is to suggest a perspective on renewing the congregation as an entity in itself and to provide tools and ways to use them in accomplishing this goal.

Part II

New Vision

2

The Need for a Vision

Passive congregations and individual methods of renewal are symptoms of the lack of an activating, mobilizing vision. For some church organizations and their leaders, vision centers on the past while others look ahead but cannot identify it. And many organizations and leaders take the easy way and substitute someone else's vision for their own unique calling.

In some groups all that is imagined is a picture of the past. There is no effort to discern the call of God. The future is unclear and their thinking about it undeveloped. As a result, they stand and do nothing. Because they have not explored the current meaning of God's presence, they lack vision and experience little of life.

In groups that look forward but cannot focus on a central vision, members seem constantly occupied. They furiously engage in all kinds of activities, but the direction of their movement is vague. The assumption is that lots of activity must be good and effective. The weakness is in failing to discern God's purpose for the particular body. The healthy calling is to focus on the wholeness of a purposeful direction.

Some groups mistakenly claim someone else's vision. The multiple renewal methods listed in chapter 1 are often ways of acting out such detached vision. Another's vision is meant for a different time, place, ethnic group, or faith commitment. It cannot merely be transplanted and adopted by others. Groups that operate in this fashion become unauthentic, unrooted. They become detached from their faith, from their context, or from their calling. Vision must *originate* in the particular body itself.

Vision, as the concept is used in this book, is a glimpse of that to which God is calling people. To have vision is to preview what is ahead but this foresight does not necessarily predetermine events. To imagine— to formulate an image before oneself—does not limit the future. A variety of constraints may alter what is perceived as one moves closer or looks further. Imaginative vision does, however, anticipate the future through the recognition that God grants creative gifts to people and also blesses them with hope. People will be energized as dreaming creates a new reality.

The envisioning of God's movement in our world provides the opportunity for all—individually and in leadership groups—to be active in a revelation. To glimpse it and to respond by moving toward God and other people is to engage in the ever-emerging realm of God. To try to understand and be active in the glimpse which God offers is to span the chasm between the ordinary and the extraordinary, God's intention and our reality, the future and the present, possibilities and unnecessary limits, faith and hopelessness. The New Testament parables of the Reign of God offer such visions of peace and justice. God's intention and one's way of life in relationship to it are illumined by the Bible.

A marvelous vision appears in the Old Testament book of Ezekiel. In chapter 37 the reader views a valley of dry and separated bones that begin to breathe and rise to their feet. The spirit of the Lord tells the prophet—and the contemporary interpreter—that the bones are the whole house of Israel, which is in exile in Babylon. Many asked if the bones could live. The oracle promises resurrection to the community. The power of God is known in human history.

This passage from the Old Testament, in which dry bones come to life, opens people's eyes to the Spirit of God empowering the ordinary. The Spirit provides new life or revitalization. That which is old can become new again through the breath of Yahweh. Perception of God's vision can bring about vitality and activity. It is God's doing—then and now—but it also involves the prophet and the multitude.

There are many post-biblical examples of vision. Dr. Martin Luther King, Jr., revealed his dream for others to see. His vision and description of healthy racial diversity have rallied and focused multitudes of people since his famous "I Have a Dream" speech given on August 28, 1963, before some 200,000 people who had marched on Washington. King's capacity to describe his vision continues to equip others to become a part of what he saw.

Vision can also be miraculous in its healing power. Doctors Carl and Stephanie Simonton are among the pioneers in the domain of mind-body communication. Some cancer patients find visualization, actually seeing what is there, to be lifesaving and life-extending. In conjunction with standard medical procedures, a vision of healing has been shown to contribute to the health of patients. To see is to believe. To focus upon what is hopeful positively affects the present and the future.

What is the impact of having a vision? It is found in preparedness and fulfillment, the offspring of vision. Careful preparation for a journey is a metaphor for development of vision. People take various approaches to life's journeys, both actual and figurative. Some throw a few things together and head off in whatever direction feels best. One family, at the last moment before their vacation trip, draws a route number from a hat and follows that road wherever it leads them. The results of such a venture may be exciting, but such trips are not to be touted as examples of group leadership. Expectations of a journey are what cause its anticipation to be a joy, its activity to include many people, and its eventuality to be fulfilling. Without a vision of the journey a traveler cannot plan for time, money, companions, reservations, and supplies. Like the best of vacations, visions lived out are full of surprises and unforeseen developments. While most memories are quite different from the visions which preceded them, imagination was the driving force. To look ahead, with others, and to follow that vision is to be drawn clearly into appropriate corporate activity.

Who is responsible for vision? The theory of revitalization presented in this book relies heavily on cooperative processes involving many people. Even the act of envisioning must be public and corporate. Yet the responsibility must be lodged initially with the leadership of a church. The initial phase must involve leaders. A primary task for those who are elected or ordained is to develop vision, publicly yoke to that vision those to whom they are responsible, and cause the vision to grow and guide a community of people that continues to make the vision its own. The envisioning activity of leaders is meant to activate and guide a group through a process of healthy change, always encouraging that body to adapt the original vision. Wise leaders will not try to do all the decision making for others nor will they vicariously carry on other segments of the spiritual life for faithful people.

Most of the initial content of vision is protected from details of program development and implementation. Involvement in work that results from vision activates additional people. Therefore, the content of initial vision has primarily to do with leadership processes cultivating activation, making commitments, and utilizing resources. Reverting back to the comparison of the development of a vision to planning for a trip, the initial content of a leadership vision includes sample descriptions of the destination as well as maps illustrating possible and recommended routes. Like a good travel agent, wise leaders prepare adequately so that others can join in the journey and make it their own. Just as an entirely preordained trip is likely to meet only the needs of the travel agent, so an overly detailed vision will not significantly involve growing numbers of people.

This book attempts to contribute a vision of and tools for a Christianized church. This section continues with visions of healthy, whole congregations, of active leadership, and of appropriately public processes.

3

Active Congregations—A Holistic Approach

What happens when those who desire to transform congregational life begin to realize that the congregation is the problem rather than clergy, leaders, liturgy, or some other aspect of the church? What happens to theory and a strategy of renewal when the real target is the congregation? The theory and strategy in this book are based on the assumption that if congregational vitality is desired, then the only meaningful target is the membership.

Denominational agencies have certainly suspected for some time that problems of congregational life are usually broader and deeper than one person—the minister. In fact, such perceptions have led to the design and advocacy of leadership development for laity. Even clergy complain about the lack of good leadership and urge their members to participate in such programs. But can the problems of congregational life be attributed solely to the lack of adequate leadership? Are not congregations so complex and dynamic that no person or group can be held responsible for their problems?

As stated earlier, the authority, responsiveness, and capacity of leaders are influenced by the state of the congregation. When goals are clear and a sizable segment of the congregation has some degree of commitment to them, the community can hold leadership accountable; further, congregations and nominating committees can exercise more discrimination in selecting people who can assist the entire membership in achieving those goals.

How can a congregation evaluate its purpose and direction, its quality of life, and its relationship to the community around it? What do leaders and clergy need in order to activate, mobilize, and transform a congregation—to enable dry bones to breathe so that Christian faith is more profoundly expressed in congregational life?

Leaders need a mandate from the congregation in order to revitalize their church. They also need a vision and tools that will enable them to activate it, so that clear goals are formulated and people are identified who can work with their leaders to accomplish these ends.

A congregational mandate is crucial. Activating a congregation means more movement as members express their concerns, personal goals for the congregation, and perceptions of the effectiveness of present leadership. Involvement—both positive and negative—will be increased. The initial response of many persons may be to dump concerns, gripes, and past experiences, but activation eventually increases their positive expectations. The congregation begins to believe that things will be different in the future. They begin to imagine that future and to work toward it. However, unless some conditions improve, the future will bring increased judgment on both leaders and the congregation itself. Unless leaders have secured a mandate for activation, they will bear the blame for any failures that do occur. Thus, leaders need a vision of the congregation as a whole and tools that will enable them to attain a mandate from the congregation. Some members are so loaded with memories of past experiences, personal vendettas, and family feuds that they cannot free themselves until an activated congregation surrounds them with a vision, vitality, and concrete evidence that change is not an illusion.

Wise leaders will deal effectively with the hopes and concerns of all members, not just of the few with whom they agree. They will design and implement processes that activate the entire congregation as it assesses the quality of its life, and its relationship to the community. A congregation is not energized when clergy or lay leaders tell members what they ought to be and do. Activation occurs on the terms of those who are activated, not the activators. For the most part, leaders do not know the terms or conditions that need to exist for congregational motivation. They may have some ideas, but they probably have little accurate knowledge about what conditions should exist so that members will be able to increase their involvement in the ministry and mission of the church.

Most strategies are based on an assumption that in a renewed congregation members must believe and do what clergy or leaders tell them. They must support one mission project and oppose another. They must undergo sensitivity training and be "one of us." They must be members of the congregation for five or ten years before they have a right to suggest new ideas and participate in leadership. The concept of activation used in this book and in working with congregations is based on seven very different assumptions:

1. God's people have all been created as worthy and talented. The gifts, vocation, and vision of each of God's people are to be seen as blessings and as vehicles for the ministry of the church. As God calls individuals into community, it is essential that leaders value them and work to affirm the potential offerings of all and stimulate responses to the possibilities God has created through them. Leaders must awake to the reality that God's grace moves in, through, and among God's people.

2. Church members have a commitment to Jesus Christ, to the Christian faith, and to the church. This commitment varies enormously in quality and quantity, and it is dynamic—capable of expanding and contracting under different conditions. The sources of commitment—Jesus Christ, Christian faith, the church as the living body of Christ—are interpreted and expressed in multiple ways. Renewal of congregational life begins with present commitments, and multiple interpretations and expressions of them.

Various interpretations of sources and the commitments flowing from them should be viewed positively. When these become public others can know, understand, and act. Further, when they are visible, the people holding them can examine them together, criticize, affirm, and transform them into something of more value and of greater meaning. When commitments are private, the energy and resources for renewal are withheld. However, when commitments are made public, they can more easily expand or contract as people, including the holders, scrutinize them.

3. Church members intend to express their commitment to Jesus Christ, Christian faith, and the church. Intentions, like commitments, are dynamic phenomena and people express them in different ways. Generally, members' hopes for and concerns about congregational life reveal their intentions in a concrete form, which can be acted upon if encouragement is provided. Renewal of congregational life is enhanced by designing effective processes that allow people to express their intentions, examine them with others in public, and act upon them.

However, a resolution to express Christian faith can be easily thwarted by leadership styles, structure, and the decision-making processes. The climate of a congregation encourages or discourages the expression of personal commitment. When intention is fragile it can be easily smothered or thwarted by internal conditions.

The forms of ministry and mission that members use to express their commitments are learned but they also have histories. Most had been appropriate some time in the past. There are, however, few occasions when the appropriateness of old structures for new conditions can be discussed with openness, candor, and informed judgment. Most persons are unaware of the historical conditions that led to the development of past modes of ministry and mission, and they are equally ignorant about the meaning of these forms. Renewal of congregational life depends upon processes that help people follow through on their intentions to express Christian faith. These same procedures must create the possibility for individuals to explore the meaning of the forms of ministry and mission they elect to follow.

4. Congregations can establish priority goals if leadership groups will create equipping processes. Congregations are capable of making hard decisions and discriminating judgments with appropriate guidance. Even members whose goals are given low priority or are omitted altogether may increase their involvement in a congregation if they feel that their commitments are acknowledged and that their leader's intentions are honest and open. Members can live with a "no" answer if they have been encouraged to participate. Once congregational goals are discovered, then leadership groups can make plans which will enable the congregation to set priorities. Church members then will vest sufficient power and authority in their leadership that their goals can be effectively accomplished.

5. Leadership groups (such as sessions, councils, and administrative boards) will budget money, time, skills, and other resources to achieve goals. Further, they will thoughtfully identify and mobilize persons who have the requisite resources and who have indicated their intention and commitment to achieving the goal.

6. Leadership groups will design ways for the congregation to evaluate priority goals, the quality of congregational life, and the effectiveness of leadership groups, equipping the membership to achieve its ministry and mission aims. Congregations need to ask: Have we accomplished anything? If we have, how well did we do? As we look back, was it worth doing? Should the goal remain a priority goal? If additional resources had been provided, would the goal have been reached more effectively? Where would the additional resources have come from? Were there additional people who could have been mobilized? Shall another goal be eliminated and the remaining resources shifted?

7. The dynamic nature of human intention, the turbulence of congregations, and the rapidly changing communities require regular attempts to renew and increase the commitment of people. Skepticism and apathy are high in many congregations, while the number of active members is low. People may remain unconvinced that genuine renewing activities will take place. However, as the congregation is effective in achieving some of its goals and the congregational climate becomes more hopeful, increasing numbers will begin to participate in goal setting and evaluative procedures. Experience has shown a modest increase in the number of members participating in the processes of goal setting and in the various aspects of congregational life during the first cycle. When a congregation is clear about its purposes and directions, church

activities take on increasing significance. Liturgy, preaching, Christian education, care of members, and concern for the community are recognized as parts of a whole that help the congregation do its work and express its commitments. When congregations are not clear about their directions, resources dissipate and competition develops between various programs. One response includes programs that activate members and allow the entire congregation to organize and invest in its leaders the power and authority needed to achieve a desired end. To engage in such visionary processes is to be involved in a church "depth" movement which, unlike the church "growth" movement, begins with God's purposes, directions, and possibilities for a particular congregation.

4

Wise Leadership and Congregational Involvement

Activating Christians requires two things from leaders. First, processes must be created—data gathering, goal setting, planning, budgeting, evaluating, reflecting, and celebrating—which will attempt to revive latent, dissipated, or sagging commitments and provide occasions for vital, fresh endeavors. Such events provide new energy and vision for others. Second, congregational resources, including members, must be organized so that effective action can take place.

Before such processes can enable dry bones to live, pastors and leadership groups need to be keenly aware of congregational life. They must recognize that people do have commitments, that most congregations are passive, that current participation of members can be improved, that their own leadership style may be producing a dead or broken spirit, and that current structures and rules may be creating an immobile people. In other words, congregational life itself needs to be brought under reflection and guidance, which means that leaders must have a vision for the congregation and that they must intend to pursue it.

A leadership group that has a vision and is intentional in its goals is a critical precondition for activating a congregation. Leaders must be willing to use their powers in achieving these transforming goals. The major powers necessary to effect such an end are the ability to initiate processes, to budget, and to create new task groups and committees. Most leadership groups have this authority. They need not control congregational life but can help the members realize some new qualities and values in their life together.

There is one snag. Leaders of most of the organizations of the world are experiencing challenges to their positions, and church leaders—clergy and laity alike—are no exception. There is a great amount of frustration and tension among church leaders, and between church leaders and congregations. Leaders do not gain much satisfaction or sense of significant accomplishment. The transition from previous types of leadership to a style or styles more effective today is often painful for both clergy and laity. The substantive question is: What model of leadership is appropriate for the church today?

Patterns and functions of governance in the church have always had a direct relation to their counterparts in the larger culture. The church has never invented new systems; it has appropriated and transformed dominant patterns that surrounded it. For example, the term "kingly" has historically been used in some traditions to describe the church's leadership. This sexist and symbolically limiting term may in itself have restricted the church's vision of its decision-making possibilities and the quality of its corporate life. John Calvin understood the mission of Jesus Christ as a kingly ministry. Yet the kingship which Jesus modeled was clearly different from the sorts of royal authority with which people were familiar. The kingly role of Jesus Christ was unique compared to both those who came before and have come after him. Unfortunately, the church has often used as its model for power, not the life and work of Jesus Christ, but other familiar metaphors which often sadly mirror qualities against which Jesus stood.

In addition to this royal court image, we also find old feudal patterns lingering in the church. In Europe from the ninth until about the fifteenth centuries, the prevailing system of political organization was based on the relationship of lord to vassal, characterized by homage, service, and wardship. This pattern was reflected in the church, and some of that style is present today. Such a concentration of power is hardly a desirable model for contemporary church leadership.

As residual patterns of feudalism are challenged in the church, a managerial style is developing that needs critical examination and reflection. As an alternative to royal and feudal images, the concept of "wise rule" has been articulated as a vision of faithful leadership. This idea comes from H. Richard Niebuhr's reinterpretation of John Calvin's understanding of the kingly or governance function of Christ's ministry.

A vision of wise rule becomes clearer as we pause to reflect upon the problematic, utilitarian culture in which we live. The need for faithful leadership becomes focused as we reflect upon what Alvin Gouldner has described succinctly in *The Coming Crisis of Western Sociology:*

> A utilitarian culture then inevitably places a great stress upon winning and losing, upon success and failure as such, rather than upon the character of the intention that shapes a person's course of action or upon the conformity of his intention with a pre-established rule or model of propriety . . .
>
> From the standpoint of utilitarian culture, it is not some transcendental standard above men, but men themselves and their own nature that become the measure. Things assume utility in relation to men, to their interests and happiness. To evaluate men or things in terms of their

consequences is to evaluate them in terms of how they may be used to pursue an interest, rather than of what they are in themselves or because they may be deemed good in their own right. Things are good or evil not in themselves but in whether they produce agreeable outcomes (65, 16).

Most primary assumptions about congregations as organizations have their source in utilitarianism. Leadership in churches has been so influenced by these standards that they are now normative. Because the criteria are derived from a larger cultural perspective—and we have not had a critical stance toward those points of view—our leaders tend to behave in a utilitarian manner. Implicit within this perspective is a set of meanings for political action: the ends justify the means; control is more important than reconciliation or love or justice.

A utilitarian perspective carries within it tacit assumptions about leadership styles with implications for action and political conduct (see *The Coming Crisis of Western Sociology*, 40). Further, it presumes a certain stance toward other people. Under the influence of utilitarianism, leaders begin to see members as entities to be used, not as people having moral intention or faith commitments that must find expression if they are to have dignity and integrity. Leaders expect compliance with their own goals, interests, and commitments, and make no provision for members' needs. Participation is useful as long as there is concurrence, compliance, and economic support.

Currently, no other perspectives exist to judge, guide, or direct people to other behaviors. Rule in the church demands the development of alternatives to utilitarianism, with concomitant leadership styles and governing behaviors. Developing other methods depends on transforming leadership and congregational life from "use" orientation to the vision of moral intent and morally appropriate methods that has characterized Christianity from its origin. An inquiry about wise rule must begin with a critical stance in relation to the utilitarian culture that dominates us and a search for the style of leadership that would reflect our moral intentions to a greater degree. Injustice in church organizations is still injustice. Misuse of persons in the church is not remedied by religious rhetoric or the word "church". An inquiry into wise rule must begin, therefore, with an assessment of our own tacit assumptions about the organizational world in which we live. We must develop an outlook which is consistent with the thought and life of Christian faith.

Present leadership must therefore give increasing attention to the quality and character of congregational life and then must assume responsibility for what it has created. The overwhelming impact of utilitarianism necessitates this. Utilitarians see church organizations and the people in them as useful and valuable only when they serve a purpose. Agendas are long and detailed for people and groups who can implement what is desired. Disagreeable and useless entities are rejected. When this happens, not only is the quality of life in the church involved, but the very nature of Christian faith is at stake.

If Christian faith is to find expression, then the challenge to wise rule is to find ways to create conditions in a church organization that encourage people to develop profound intent and to express it through the most moral methods available. The church must be at least one training ground for Christians as they move into the world. Such preparation, in addition to creating vital Christian life, provides an arena for a critique of the culture and, therefore, is resistant to utilitarian ways of being in the world.

Utilitarianism in the church has crippled our ability to love and to feel loved. It is the foundation from which mistrust, manipulation, and denial of personhood arise. Personal qualities such as courage, hope, justice, patience, and tenderness, which have worth in themselves, are not valued. Wise rule begins with the assumption that rule itself is a moral activity that concretely expresses faith. No moral ends justify immoral methods of manipulation, calculation, and alienation. Leadership is needed that can search out its own moral intent, delve into the meanings of Christian doctrines—both for the work of governing and for congregational life—and express these meanings in its own way.

Further, leadership is needed that can enable members of the church to look at the quality and character of their intentions and at the meaning of Christian faith to them. Such guidance can assist them—through the discovery and provision of morally appropriate methods—to express themselves. Leaders must take the members of a congregation seriously, and assume that they have a working Christian faith. They are seen as a public that can be morally intentional and responsible when processes of governance are created that encourage their effective participation.

Leadership is needed that can help a congregation think about its life, its faith commitments, its relationship to the community, and its care of its own members and their families. Guidance is needed to activate the faith commitments of members, help them think about the substance and quality of their commitments, and create the means whereby they can act. The activation and guidance of members with Christian commitments and intentions is the primary task of leaders. What style of leadership makes this most possible? What can appropriately replace utilitarianism in our congregations today?

"Public beneficence" is one type of leadership that may be an appropriate alternative to utilitarianism and produce those qualities needed to activate a congregation. Beneficence (a quality that leads to the conferring of benefits or that causes good to be done) is a trait expected of effective leaders. Historically, beneficent activity has been private and unexamined, with leaders meeting privately. Actions taken were not made public. Those in charge assumed they were promoting the common good, because they were elected by those who trusted them to do so.

Public beneficence suggests that the intentions and actions of leaders are open to examination by people affected by their behavior. Public beneficence means that the nature and quality of ministry by both leaders and congregation can receive the reflection and guidance of both. Together, leaders and members are responsible for their common life, and the whole congregation's witness and service, intentions and goals can be mutually scrutinized. Congregations can be publicly moral and beneficent through processes by which leaders enable the congregation to face itself and make decisions about what it sees.

This style of leadership creates the environment for the congregation to express its wisdom, its self-understanding, and its perception of how it desires to relate to the world around it. The joint public benevolence of leaders and congregation creates the possibility that a church community will confront itself and at least ask the questions: Are we providing for each other's welfare? Is this method effective? Are there other goals more worthy?

Private activity means that most people are passive and under the control of a few. Public activity means that more members tend to participate in the transformation of their own and the congregational life. To be active in a church means that people are responsible and accountable. Private processes lodge these attributes in a few individuals. The volunteer nature of the church and the nature of Christian faith, which calls individuals and congregations to accountability and responsibility to God for their lives, renders such a leadership style inappropriate. The private style functioned in previous historical periods because there was both authority and power to reward and punish members, thus insuring compliance to the desires of a few. Today, while authority is still granted in constitutions and books of church order, the punitive powers have been stripped away, making the private style ineffective.

Leadership must be public in doing good if it is to gain the trust of volunteers. Confidence and trust are the basis of legitimacy and have their own power, which is conferred on leaders. Public leadership models accountability to God and God's people. Activity based on Christian commitments creates the environment for energetic members to align themselves with that which is visible. People and groups can identify with values that are producing active leaders. Public activity makes it possible to gather and focus the energy and commitments of people and groups in a congregation. Achievement of a broad range of goals and objectives is made possible when a congregation is dynamic.

There is no simple way to activate a congregation. Private beliefs, intentions, and goals need to be transformed through public processes into visible commitments and activity. A congregation needs data-gathering and goal-setting processes to encourage reflection by members about the direction of congregational life. These processes should enable members to become more sensitive to actual conditions in their church and their community. Activating members depends on raising up these individuals' Christian values for clarification, questioning, and affirmation. This enables members to reflect upon the meaning of their own values for congregational life.

Leaders point to values represented in Christian symbols and they encourage reflection on these in church groups. Those who engage in wise rule and guide others toward public beneficence understand that the active congregation is one whose values are more fully examined than are those in passive surroundings. Leaders investigate points where values and their symbols can be brought together for reflection.

Christian values are mediated not only through words, but through a congregation's structure, decision making, and communication processes. Congregational life communicates values. Structures and processes symbolize and actualize these values. Therefore, leaders should search for that structure and those processes that embody Christian values most powerfully and that will enable a congregation to be responsible and accountable. The basis of public beneficence is a set of social processes and a structural reality that express Christian values. This undergirding is not a metaphysical, a psychological, or a rational doctrine, but a concrete vision of life in Christ. The foundation must be present in the everyday concerns of a people in order for the passive to become active, for dry bones to live.

There are three identifiable elements in such a strategy of activation, which seem appropriate to a leadership style of public beneficence:

1. Actions of leaders work toward congregational wholeness and effectiveness. Committees, task groups, and boards are seen as parts of a whole, which must contribute to the whole. Leaders guide congregational units to increasingly serve the needs of the entire congregation.
2. Leaders use data gathering, goal setting, planning, evaluating, and training to guide the task groups, committees, and boards toward realization of the congregation's values in church and community life. They create structures and processes that actively move a congregation toward the achievement of these values.
3. Guiding actions by leaders use processes that increase the cohesiveness of the congregation around shared values and norms. Oral communication—in contrast to written contact—is the primary means for developing cohesiveness.

    Leaders use consensus in developing the commitment to shared values and norms. This does not mean that decisions are made by cooperative congregational opinion, but that processes are used to identify goals based on Christian values in order to mobilize members, and increase cohesiveness. Finally, leaders provide accurate information about their own activity; about conditions in the congregation, community, and larger church and world; and about the progress or failure anticipated in achieving the common aim. Through valid and reliable information, members can assess their own beliefs and activity in relation to the meaning provided by leaders.

Guidance toward fresh vitality is the leader's major task. A vital, active membership is one sign God is at work among God's people. Leaders have the responsibility of activating the people in God's service. Public beneficence of leaders, manifest in an activated congregation, requires new, public processes that will promote a fresh morality in congregational life.

5

Public Processes and Public Morality

There is a double meaning to the word *public* as we use it. In the first sense it means that which is visible and open to the scrutiny, criticism, and modification of others. Public processes are those that are known and can be examined. Both moral appropriateness and effectiveness in eliciting the moral intent of others can be evaluated and judged by those who participate in them. People can know and make judgments about their participation in processes designed by someone else.

In the second sense *public* means that the processes are designed for larger groups, for congregations or segments of congregations, and that the values, commitments, feelings, and perceptions of these people are revealed to others. The emphasis is on processes whereby a congregation looks at itself and makes discriminating judgments.

Our emphasis on public processes and morality contrasts with the private processes and morality of the recent past. This alteration of emphasis is based on the New Testament image of the body of Christ, and the Old Testament emphasis on the people of God. Much of the Old Testament is a record of speeches and judgments against the whole people, the tribe, the collective group. The Israelites are called to repentance. They are judged, loved, shown mercy and kindness, and destroyed as a nation of tribes, not as individuals. Individuals are condemned for leading God's people astray, but it is the people who are expected to be faithful. Even bad leaders are not a sufficient excuse for the wickedness of the people.

The New Testament also uses corporate imagery. The church is a collective people called for God's work. It is a holy nation, a royal priesthood, the New Israel, the body of Christ. This people is corporately—not individually—responsible to God for its life of love and service.

The very nature of the church as a body means that both its methods and morals must be visible to itself and others. The church is called to be a publicly faithful and moral people. However, this scriptural emphasis on the people of God and the body of Christ has been largely ignored. Private morality has been stressed, a type of morality not open to scrutiny of its method, intent, or content. Private morality remains vested in individuals and small groups. The assumption has been that privately moral organizations, would be publicly moral.

This assumption is not true. Organizations are not mere collections of "good" individuals. They are entities in themselves, which may or may not show love, justice, acceptance, and care in their lives. Thus, a group of individually moral people does not necessarily create or make a moral congregation. Congregations have goals, structures, political processes, rules, and procedures that create an environment that ultimately expresses something of what God is about in God's world. Private morality does not acknowledge the ways in which God holds God's people accountable for their corporate life. It is a one-sided, truncated, heretical version of both the New Testament community of faithful people and the Old Testament people of the covenant.

Congregations must be public—open, visible, and available, both to their own members and those outside their church—if they are to be faithful to their source and nature. Christians are groups of publicly concerned people who look at the quality and character of their own life. They are concerned, as John Calvin suggested, about "the Gospel in the Church." This public interest in corporate life is visible to those outside. In a concrete sense, this is evangelism, the sharing of good news. The discerning look of a congregation as it carries out its witness and service is verification that it has a moral intent that it seeks to express. If there is no gospel among the church's people, there is no evangelism. Good news in the New Testament sense is not empty words, but a life of faithfulness between God and God's people.

Areas of congregational life for which public processes may be designed and implemented to assist the congregation in its efforts to assess itself are:

—Goals, i.e., nature, quality, worthiness, and direction
—Worship
—Leadership
—Structure
—Decision-making and communication processes
—Political style and activity
—Relation to the community
—Involvement in mission
—Relationships of the different programs, projects, and parts
—Education
—Climate, character, or internal environment

The above areas are aspects of congregational life that change in response to new perceptions of faithfulness, changing membership, and fluctuating communities. Each congregation, as a constantly changing public body, is in continuing need of valid information about the quality and character of its own life, as well as information about the community in which it exists. It needs information it can use as a basis for critical reflection about its life, and upon which it can act with confidence. Public methods of obtaining information are needed so that congregations can examine them to decide whether or not they will produce valid information. It is important that congregations gain confidence in the leadership that has designed such methods and, ultimately, in themselves as responsive and responsible people. When information and the sources of information are not trusted, confidence and responsiveness are diminished.

A lack of valid information for a congregation means it will have little possibility of discovering the truth about itself as a corporate body. Faithfulness to God depends upon truthfulness in dealing with God, church members, and the world in which the church is placed. Faithfulness to God's calling is manifest when the people are candid about the character and quality of their corporate life, and when there is responsiveness to what the church discovers about itself. The prophetic call of Jesus and the Old Testament prophets was a call to be responsive to the truth about the character and quality of life among God's people. Public processes and public morality, as method and response, have a long history in Christianity. The numerous reforming moments in the history of the church are vivid testimony to the power and appropriateness of both public processes and public morality. In the next chapter we will examine these in relation to activation of a congregation.

Part III

Public Involvement and Activation

6

An Overview of Modes of Public Involvement

Seldom in church history have leaders intentionally and critically examined ways in which members publicly participate in the church. In those rare moments when attention has been given to participation, those processes have frequently been related to systems of discipline and to the courts. Much has been written, for instance, on the number of witnesses and types of evidence needed in trials for all manner of offenses, ranging from adultery to begging without a license. More recently, civil legislation has taken from church courts and governing bodies the responsibility for administering justice and minding the morals of communities.

Today there is a need to reexamine the ways in which members publicly participate in the life of the church. Many of the meanings and descriptions of participation procedures, which are embedded and encrusted in by-laws and constitutions, were written when the church had a different role in society and quite different expectations for its members. Today church leadership expects members to be active—except for those few remaining feudal lords and knights of the Round Table who still think benevolent autocracy is possible. However, when they try to achieve this end, leaders and leadership groups are often victimized by the intent, meaning, and design of method they have inherited.

Processes designed to create opportunities and guide people in their church participation are also ways in which members are defined in the church; they are, in a real sense, a definition of the "gospel in the church." Those who design the processes reveal their own values and expectations to all who will take part in them, as an examination of the meetings of any congregation's governing bodies and committees will show. The time set for meetings, agenda, leadership style, preparation of participants, record keeping, and resources available are exceptionally powerful expressions of the intent of leaders who design meetings for others. The intent is experienced and interpreted by members.

Critical appraisal of present processes and the restructuring of processes for future meetings begins with these questions:

—What is the intent of the process for people?

—What are the purposes of the meeting and the purposes to be served by how people participate?

—Is the process intended to secure ratification of a decision already made by leaders?

—Is genuine involvement and commitment to the results of the processes intended?

—Is there an expectation that new information will be shared?

—Is there an expectation that activation of people will be the result?

Answering these questions will enable leaders to discover their own assumptions and intentions for others in meetings. Leaders can then decide if the current procedures reflect only their own values. Clarity of assumptions, intentions, and purposes can lead to creating more humane gatherings that more substantially reflect Christian values.

Leaders and members may differ sharply over the intent of participation in processes. When members share information, make choices, and respond to the decisions of their leaders, the intent needs to be as clear as possible and must be reflected in the design. Leaders and members may expect too much from inherited processes that were not designed to withstand social change. More initiative, activity, and resources are expected from people in our society than in the past. Yet the church assumes that members are passive, dependent, or ignorant. And today, Christian faith is defined as more than something to be believed; the good news it proclaims is something other than a blissful "next life" after a miserable earthly existence. The doctrines of faith are directed toward this world, where hope, reconciliation, joy, promise, and fulfillment of the gospel have profound meaning for all human activity, and particularly for practices within the church.

The design and implementation of processes in the church are major practical tasks for leaders and require the best theological reflection possible. Let us look, therefore, at various measures for encouraging congregational involvement and evaluate their effectiveness.

Public Self-Assessment

Self-assessment is the public process of obtaining valid information about the congregation, or some aspect of its life, and making discriminating judgments about the implications of that information. Public self-assessment implies that the public examines its life—or an aspect of its life—makes judgments about what it sees, and engages in action to create better conditions. Valid self-assessment leads to action in order to deal with the truth the people have discovered about themselves. Otherwise the people will live in untruth, knowing that conditions exist that should be changed. Truthfulness, as theologian Hans Küng has pointed out, is a paramount sign of Christian faith at work in the church.

There are two types of self-assessment: descriptive and prescriptive. Descriptive self-assessment resembles taking a snapshot of the entire congregation or of a particular part, program, or activity. It is a searching look at the way in which the congregation presently expresses its Christian faith. Descriptive self-assessment involves looking at the perceptions the congregation has about itself and its relationship to the surrounding community. This kind of self-assessment says, We look like this. Do we like the way we look? If we do not like what we see, what changes can we make to alter the picture?

Prescriptive self-assessment is an evaluative appraisal of the congregation or of some aspect of its life. This style of assessment assumes some value, theological perspective, or understanding of ministry and mission. It creates an idea or word-picture of what the congregation should be doing, believing, and/or thinking, and evaluates the congregation in this light. A prescriptive assessment says, This is how a Christian congregation should look. Do we resemble this picture? Do we like what we see? Should we give thanks and celebrate? What will we do if our picture does not compare favorably with the word-picture?

If this latter style is to be an activating process, two equally important steps are involved: First, there must be agreement by leaders and members on the word-picture to be used as the basis for an evaluative assessment. Clergy or lay leaders cannot impose a word-picture on a congregation and realistically expect it to be used. Such a picture will only be helpful when members themselves decide that it is appropriate for their use. Leaders can suggest criteria for developing a picture that would be appropriate, and they can design the process of reflection through which the congregation discusses its word-picture with its leaders. If a congregation is to engage in genuine evaluative self-assessment, members must commit themselves to the evaluation before it takes place.

Second, a process that utilizes the evaluative word-picture must be designed and implemented. This process should include opportunities for proposing ways to bring about congruence between the word-picture and the actual conditions found in the congregation. These steps for carrying out priority goals and making changes in response to either descriptive or prescriptive assessments will probably require altering structures, communication, and decision-making processes, as well as rules and procedures for doing the work. Means to these ends include increased discretion, negotiation, and systematic planning.

Goal Setting

A current trend within the church is that of goal setting—a designation that means many things with respect to the purposes and involvement of members. Many congregations have established goals and achieved nothing of consequence. A survey of the different meanings of goal setting may help leaders clarify their intent. Three inadequate processes are outlined below.

1. Goal setting based on community studies and surveys has been an important process for many congregations. Leaders assign members the task of obtaining information about the community and then propose goals based on the information obtained. The study committee communicates recommendations to the governing board, which in turn makes a decision on whether or not to implement each of the recommendations. The task of mobilizing the volunteers and resources needed and gaining congregational support for the decisions comes next. When the level of trust in leaders is low, the suggestions become diverse and controversial; additional resources are needed, and there is likely to be great resistance to the whole process. Thus, the congregation will not be activated.
2. Frequently leaders attempt to establish goals for themselves and the congregation on an annual retreat. Leaders must "sell" their product and mobilize members who have the time, energy, and money to achieve the goals. This task is exceptionally difficult, and such negotiations are usually unsuccessful.
3. Another method of goal setting has been to invite members to share ideas through questionnaires or leader "listening" sessions. Moderators tabulate the information and then attempt to establish congregational goals. They also have the problem of "selling" their interpretations and formulations. Minimal activation takes place.

Each process of goal setting involves leaders and members in different ways and includes different expectations for both. But most of the procedures expect minimum involvement of members until endorsement of the leader's work is required. This ratifying process does not activate or mobilize; it is political and legitimates work already done.

Legitimization, however, is dynamic and varies in degrees of completeness. Most ratifying processes result in little support for establishing goals, allocating resources, altering roles of clergy and/or laity, increasing the budget, and like matters, because those asked to sanction the decisions had not been involved in making them. In a turbulent and diverse environment, processes that produce maximum legitimization are needed. Otherwise leaders will sense the low level of approval for their work and will respond by doing nothing or by making minimal responses to the various claims made upon them. Leaders gain power and authority through intensive and extensive processes which activate members behind common congregational goals. The power and authority to act is bestowed on leaders when members see that leaders can be trusted to assist the congregation in achieving the goals which have been established in public processes, where both members and leaders are held accountable.

Altering the design of congregational life is essential in implementing goals and responding to self-assessment. If new organizational arrangements are not created, the goals, priorities, and organizational conditions of the present congregation will remain. If outmoded methods are not altered, no substantive response to goal setting or self-assessment will be made. The response is only one of words—goal statements printed in the church bulletin and annual report—and self-assessment remains only a word-picture of how a congregation should look.

Evaluative Processes

Evaluative processes provide information to the congregation about its achievements, the quality of its life, and the degree to which the results of activities and programs have matched its vision and sense of mission. Two types of evaluative processes have been used in congregations: end-product and in-process.

End-product evaluation answers the questions: Did we do what we said we were going to do? Is the result what we expected?

In-process evaluation seeks to provide answers to the questions: Do we know that we are on the correct path? How far have we come in achieving our goal? Are we where we should be at this time?

Evaluative processes are public in several ways. Evaluation is a visible activity, and criteria used in this process are open to public criticism. Assessment is done by those who act and those who are the recipients of that action. The results are made known to the congregation. Every aspect is open for scrutiny in order to learn how well the whole and its parts—as expressions of the ministry of people in God's service—are responsive to the claims of Christian faith.

Training of Leaders and Members

The first step in leadership training is to assist those involved in activating a congregation around common goals. When a congregation has aims that are important to it, then leaders can be trained to enable the congregation to achieve them. Yet most leadership training programs are based on the assumption that the major problem of an apathetic, ineffective congregation is its leadership. A congregation without purpose will not elect leadership that will establish bold new directions. Mobilized congregations tend to produce energized leaders who feel compelled to receive training and are responsive to it because they know they have a congregational mandate.

In the past, leadership training has been conducted by special interest groups of denominational agencies—for example, Christian education, stewardship, and evangelism committees. The congregation was divided into specialized areas, and leaders were trained for these areas. No one taught them how to mobilize whole congregations or how to assist them in achieving their goals. Each special interest group has assumed it knew the objectives of the congregation and trained its leaders to achieve those particular ends. Consequently, the overall intentions of congregations themselves have been ignored or subverted.

One example is sufficient to make the point. Most congregations have Christian education committees which purport to be concerned with the total educational needs of a congregation. These committees have been trained to be responsive primarily to Sunday church school needs, and the congregation's priority educational goals in the areas of worship, care of members, and mission in the community are largely ignored.

To train leaders effectively to work on all priority goals, a Christian education committee must ask: What are the educational needs in relation to the new priority congregational goals? It is conceivable that such a committee would not even have the church school on its agenda, while it focuses on the congregation's new objectives!

Leadership training is a response to the public processes of goal setting, congregational self-assessment, and evaluation. In addition, it is a public process that focuses on the needs of leaders, and they themselves subject it to scrutiny and critical reflection.

For the past fifty years, theologians have written extensively about the nature of the church and its ministry. Their writing has had direct consequences for both clergy and laity seeking self-understanding and a definition of their roles. Contemporary theology, with its renewed emphasis on the people of God, the body of Christ, and the corporate nature of church and ministry, has called for a much more active, educated, reflective laity. This has meant that ministers are no longer "the church" and cannot minister solely on its behalf. Nor can they engage in rules with the same patterns of authority and power as before. Contemporary theology and the trend to democratize institutions have fused to raise important questions about the roles of clergy and laity.

The results of this coalescence can be seen in congregations where some people refer to the minister in formal terms as Herr Pastor, Preacher, "Senior" Pastor, or The Minister, while others may use his or her first name. Some members want the minister to be a model for the congregation, while others expect behavior that is no more or no less than they expect of themselves. The conflict can be seen most clearly in members' various expectations in regard to the clergy's duties. The tasks of preaching, calling, and pastoral care rank high for some members. Teaching small groups and personal involvement with members in community issues would rank high for others. In addition, clergy have their own values, priorities, and role definition, which may or may not coincide with those of the members. Much of the conflict in congregations is due to these disparate and incongruent expectations.

Therefore, one aspect in most strategies of congregational renewal is role clarification. For some theorists and practitioners, this process is a major component of renewal, but it is actually secondary to the major problem—disparity of goals.

Role clarification is of little use to a congregation that has common goals, self-assessment measures, an organizational design, evaluation methods, and training programs to help leaders and members participate more effectively in accomplishing those tasks that are important to them. When a congregation has definite goals, there can be an explicit emphasis on the skills, competencies, and knowledge needed to help it accomplish them. For a directionless organization, role clarification is useless.

A Summary of a Perspective and Processes for Activating Congregations

A commitment to public processes means that the assumptions, perspectives, and hypotheses about what we expect to happen must be accessible to others. Most theories and strategies for change are privately held, based upon assumptions that cannot be examined, and that are suspected of being highly manipulative.

One of the most important constraints in working with congregations has been the suspicion by members that non-members are "agents" of the minister, presbytery, diocese, synod, or conference, which is making yet another attempt to change them. Ministers have suspected that the presbytery executive, synod president, conference superintendent, or bishop are conspiring to do something—as yet unknown—to them. The hidden assumptions and the private, unexamined, and frequently manipulative methods of the past have made it extremely difficult for ministers and congregations to recognize and accept differences.

Outsiders working with a congregation have shown us that non-members using the theory and processes described here can effectively assist congregations to become more vital in ministry and mission. Leaders of a congregation who understand these premises may use them without the aid of an expert and achieve substantially the same results. It is important also for people who will make decisions about processes and participate in them to know as much as possible about them. Effectiveness is enhanced through increased understanding.

A summary of assumptions about congregations, possible change processes to be initiated by leaders, and expected outcomes is shown in

Table 1. The succeeding chapters will contain fuller descriptions and illustrations of methods used in congregations. While instruments and techniques actually used in congregation will be presented, their purpose is to provide leaders with the resources they need to design their own ways of increasing the participation of members. Processes should be designed for a particular congregation. No material presented in this book should be used without adapting the language and steps to the unique needs and context of the congregation. For example, conditions of distrust and alienation require more consideration, with much greater care given to assurance of openness and faithfulness in dealing with information. In congregations with a high level of trust, some steps can be eliminated and the period of implementation can be shortened. Leaders will need to ask continually: For whom are we designing this process? What are the actual conditions in the congregation? How do members view us? Do they trust us to design and conduct these studies? If not, what additional steps must be included to develop that trust?

Processes for people cannot be simply invented. The design and implementation is an act of ministry that requires the love, justice, kindness, and reflectiveness of leaders. Used mechanically, they are a repudiation of ministry. It is essential that leaders acquire the tools to enrich their congregations, and that they not use the resources provided in this book uncritically.

Table 1 A Perspective on Activating Congregations

Assumptions About Congregations	Change Processes Which May Be Used by Leaders to Be Responsive to Assumptions	Change Behaviors and Conditions Expected in Congregations
A. The Congregation is affected by its environment.	Public goal-setting processes.	Changes in relation of congregation to environment.
There is a relationship, which is either positive or negative as the environment influences a congregation.	Public self-assessment processes. Organizational design to achieve goals more effectively. Evaluation processes.	Increased programs and activities to respond to community conditions. New goals for congregations.

Assumptions About Congregations	Change Processes Which May Be Used by Leaders to Be Responsive to Assumptions	Change Behaviors and Conditions Expected in Congregations
There is an effect on the internal life of the congregation, its climate, purpose, goals, and organizational design.		New personnel to achieve goals. Improved organizational arrangement. Mobilization of resources—human, financial, skills, energy, ideas, time.
B. A congregation is a meaning system in which there are: —Personal meanings. —Diverse theological commitments. —Diverse interest and concerns. —Diverse social involvements.	Public goal-setting processes which allow organization to know and act upon the following: —Individual goals for self in congregations. —Individual goals for congregation. —Congregational goals.	New goals for: —Organization. —People in the organization. Change in relationship of individuals and groups to the congregation. New coalitions and cooperation among groups.
C. A congregation is composed of interdependent systems: —Communication systems.	Public self-assessment processes. Public goal-setting processes. Organizational design.	New communication networks, processes, and style of commnication among leaders and members. Changes in political decision-making processes.

(Continued on following page)

Assumptions About Congregations	Change Processes Which May Be Used by Leaders to Be Responsive to Assumptions	Change Behaviors and Conditions Expected in Congregations
—Political decision-making systems.	Training.	Polity revisions—changes in rules and procedures which enable people to be more effective in living their Christian commitments.
—Program systems.	Program resourcing in areas of organization's priority goals. Evaluation.	Program alterations, including new programs and discontinuation of old programs which are no longer priority goals.
D. The congregation has a structure—an arrangement of people and resources in time and space in patterns of relationships and differentiation, according to goals, tasks, interests, and needs.	Organizational design of structure which facilitates goals of groups and persons in congregations. Evaluation.	More facilitating organizational arrangements. Altered locations of decision making, people, resources, programs, etc.
E. Congregation is a historical entity which has:	Public goal-setting processes.	Alteration of role of traditional:
—Traditional modes of behavior. —Traditional norms.	Public self-assessment of influence of history and tradition on organizational goals and people.	—Beliefs. —Norms. —Modes of behavior.

Assumptions About Congregations	Change Processes Which May Be Used by Leaders to Be Responsive to Assumptions	Change Behaviors and Conditions Expected in Congregations
—Traditional beliefs. —Historical experiences, both positive and negative, which have affected a congregation's thinking about itself, its program, and its imagining the future.		More effective use of historical strengths and assessment of constraining effect that these impose on mission and ministry today.
F. Organization has roles for: —Laity, which are influenced by age, sex, income, education, status, prestige, etc. —Clergy, which conform to particular historical interpretations of the ministry, including priestly activities, prophetic activities, kingly (governance, or management) activities.	Public goal-setting processes. Public self-assessment. Organizational design. Role clarification. Evaluation.	Role changes of clergy and laity. New definitions and locations of responsibilities, according to goals, task skills, and competence needed by a congregation to achieve its purposes.

7

Public Self-Assessment Processes

Both persons and groups have feelings, perceptions, and knowledge that affect participation in congregational life. Regardless of whether their understanding is fully accurate, people act with what knowledge they have, which is usually biased and inaccurate. And they make their evaluations on the basis of their perceptions.

Public self-assessment processes attempt to equip people to identify their feelings, perceptions, and knowledge and spot ways to alter the conditions that produced them. For example, leaders of congregations may note apathy or ill will among members, low attendance at meetings, or expressions of frustration, resentment, and hostility by individuals and groups. Self-assessment processes can help detect reasons for such behaviors and suggest alternative responses and conditions that may lead to improvement.

Increased vitality can develop in a congregation when members look together at some part of their life, make judgments, and work to find alternative conditions and programs. In public processes, members can share what they see, know, or feel about what is taking place, and then reflect together about the accuracy of their perceptions. They can share information with others for validation or correction and can develop alternatives to present practice and conditions.

Perceptions of congregational life are sometimes affected by the effectiveness of communication and the relationships between people and groups. Misperception or inadequate understanding suggests communication problems. These are difficulties that can be solved when leaders know what is causing them. Frequently, too, problems arise because members do not know certain facts about congregational life. Ignorance of conditions, programs, and actions taken may produce alienation, negative feelings, and disruption, even when members have satisfying relationships and excellent communication systems.

Leaders cannot activate others. Members activate themselves. Those in charge can model behaviors appropriate for members or lead charismatically. Ultimately it is the member who decides to increase her or his involvement and participate more fully in congregational ministry and mission. The task of leaders is to help create the conditions under which members will decide to activate themselves. Public self-assessment enables identification of current or past conditions that created inactive members and helps cite new conditions likely to encourage people to increase their involvement. Members cooperatively assessing their own feelings, perceptions, knowledge, and evaluations can provide moderators with valid information about past and present conditions and offer fresh ideas that will enable members to live out their Christian commitments more fully.

Using Self-Assessment Instruments

Several survey instruments are provided in this chapter to illustrate different areas of congregational life that can be studied. The word *instrument* is used intentionally. These are tools which are not ends in themselves, but vital for repairing, creating, and restoring. If a tool does not assist in activating members, it should be discarded.

Because each congregation is different, self-assessment tools should be molded to a congregation's specific needs. Their thoughtful and careful creation will contribute to effective activation. Language should be tested with members to make sure the intended meaning is conveyed. Leaders who create these aids should be able to specify the end to which they are working. With prescriptive assessments it is particularly important that surveys be cooperatively designed by appropriate governing groups.

Points of Caution

The instruments on these pages are to be used in congregations only after adapting them to the specific purposes of each congregation!

Frequently, public self-assessment instruments are converted into opinion surveys, research studies, and statistical analyses by congregational researchers. The information obtained by the self-assessments should be reserved for those who give the data. These findings are their personal disclosures. When self-assessment instruments are treated as questionnaires and the information taken from members is categorized, summarized, and interpreted, the conclusions are devoid of power. Summaries and interpretations of how people and groups feel have little influence, either with members who give them or with leaders who are the recipients. Members make their own information powerful. Members must deal with their own and others' interests in the most powerful way—groups that listen and share—and encourage one another to reexamine and perhaps modify old modes of operation. Within a group there is support for making needed congregational changes. Self-change does not occur when there are only summaries of statistical data; people change in relation to others. Printed data are irrelevant to most self-changing.

Designing an instrument with a clear purpose for a particular group is only the first step in self-assessment. Such tools are designed for use in a process that leads toward activation, self-changing, and congregational change. If isolated, they become mere opinion surveys or questionnaires. The examples in this chapter are designed for use in the nine-step process outlined below, which progresses from information gathering to implementation. Self-assessment takes time. A one to three hour time period should be allotted for it to take place, depending upon the number of items in the instrument.

A Process for Using a Self-Assessment Instrument

1. The instrument should be completed by individuals.
2. A profile is developed as individuals share their responses to the instrument's questions. In groups of six to ten, they should work through the following steps to compile a group profile on each item. To do this, the group leader may request persons to raise their hands as he or she indicates the number (1–7) under each item. For example, a group profile may look like the following: (The numbers above the line indicate the number of persons in a group of eight who marked that location on their instrument.)

Fearful	1	3	1	1		2		Not fearful
	1	2	3	4	5	6	7	

3. Each group of six to ten people identifies items on the instrument for which there is a wide range of responses or on which a significant number reply negatively. These items suggest possible problem areas.
4. Each group should choose what it sees as the two or three most important items and then discuss these problem areas. As the group goes over the subject checked, it will decide whether a particular item points to a real problem, requiring a solution. The following questions may be used for each item checked: What specific experiences have you had that can help the group understand the problem? Are there others who have had similar experiences? As we look at these responses, do we conclude that this area presents difficulty for some members of the congregation?
5. The following questions will be helpful in an appraisal of the situation: What appear to be the reasons why people have these negative experiences? What causes can we identify? If we really understand what is going on, can we state the reasons in a brief paragraph and share them with others?

6. Questions can help the group formulate possible solutions to the problems: As we come to understand the experiences of some of our members, can we think of changes we could make to better care for these members? What specific conditions should be different? Does the Confession of Faith of the congregation, the Mission Statement, or the Statement of Covenant offer suggestions for solving this problem?
7. This last step is not always needed. It is included here to remind a group to pause and ask itself whether it really has the information necessary in order to proceed. Ask: Can we make a decision about the problem and find a solution? If we need additional data, what specifically must we know? How will the information be gathered? By interviews? An instrument? Who will gather it? To whom should the material be given? Since this may be the only time this particular group meets, it is important to make someone responsible for follow-up.
8. For this particular congregation, with its unique ministry and mission, which solution seems best? List the reasons that can be shared with others to enable them to understand why a particular decision was made. Conclusions should be recorded for sharing later.
9. Which people or groups should begin implementation? Do they have the needed resources? If not, what do they need, and where can it be obtained? What is a reasonable time schedule for arriving at the solution? The information from each small group should be recorded and shared with the congregation.

A major benefit of this method is the way in which opinions become graphically visualized by participants. Individuals can easily see how similar or different their ideas are from those of others. This approach also protects the anonymity of those involved, unless someone chooses to make her or his position known. Thus those reluctant to speak in large groups are heard.

In most instances the process is interrupted at step 4 and never completed. Groups have excellent discussions but never examine or implement solutions. When used properly, public self-assessment is a way to establish goals and objectives in problem areas of congregational life. Directions to be pursued must come from the process, otherwise many members will become apathetic or alienated. Leaders should plan to get to Step 9, and be ready with recommendations for implementation. If the result is only a discussion group, cynicism and increased apathy and alienation can result. Leaders should not engage the congregation in these processes unless they know that they will get definite results.

At the end of a self-assessment process, leaders should see that the results from each group are shared. Then the recommendations for implementation should be studied by the governing board. Priority among the proposals should be established, task groups appointed and training of these committees conducted. People should be recruited who are committed to implementing the designated solution. In fact, many should come from those who engaged in the self-assessment.

Self-assessment processes lead to activation of a congregation when members work with one another by sharing experiences, understanding areas of concern, and cooperatively arriving at solutions to problems. In addition leaders must be responsive to members, encouraging them to be concerned about their life as a congregation and about their relationship to the surrounding community. Caring and prophetic voices and programs can arise from many locations in a congregation—not only from the pastor and lay leaders—when processes are systematically provided to encourage them.

Descriptive Self-Assessment

In the previous chapter, descriptive self-assessment was likened to a snapshot of an organization or one of its parts, programs, or activities. That is, a corporate body looks at what is taking place in its midst. In some cases, the assessment may evoke a desire for change. The following pages present several instruments for descriptive self-assessment along with brief comments about how they may be used. (The material may be copied for use with groups.)

How Are We Working Together?

This instrument can be used in a variety of settings; some committees have used it as an annual review. Other groups have used it as a way of opening a discussion. It is not meant to be used as a statistical data-gathering device, but as a vehicle for creating conversation about important issues, which may include celebration, problems to be solved, or changes to be made. This descriptive example is meant to be generic and independent of any unique factors in the life of an organization.

How Are We Working Together?

Assess your group by rating it on a scale from 7 (ideal) to 1 (unacceptable) with respect to each of the factors. Then with the rest of the group discuss as thoroughly as possible your situation in regard to each item. Pay particular attention to those results which should be celebrated, those which average below 5, and those with a wide range of individual ratings. Formulate some ideas about why these perceptions exist. They are likely to show great diversity among the participants.

1. I feel satisfied with the group's progress so far.

Satisfied	7	6	5	4	3	2	1	Dissatisfied

2. I feel free to express my ideas.

Satisfied	7	6	5	4	3	2	1	Dissatisfied

3. I feel my ideas and opinions are heard.

Satisfied	7	6	5	4	3	2	1	Dissatisfied

4. I feel satisfied with the way decisions are made.

Satisfied	7	6	5	4	3	2	1	Dissatisfied

5. I feel there is trust and openness in this group.

Satisfied	7	6	5	4	3	2	1	Dissatisfied

6. I feel a part of the group.

Satisfied	7	6	5	4	3	2	1	Dissatisfied

7. I feel satisfied with how we are using our time.

Satisfied	7	6	5	4	3	2	1	Dissatisfied

Strength Assessment

The following assessment is designed to help a church or a committee identify its strengths, weaknesses, and its hopes for the future. In working with any group, it is important to provide conditions of psychological safety, so that people will be less reluctant to share their real feelings, ideas, and values. Therefore, this activity attempts to emphasize the positive experiences of the group and of individuals. This activity can be used as the basis of a church board's weekend retreat, a committee's self-evaluation session, a pastors' support group, an individual assessment process, a career-planning design, and in several other ways, depending on need.

Assessing Our Strengths

We usually have a hard time affirming ourselves and one another. This form of self-assessment can help us praise our strengths and it can also be a message of grace coming before law. It is not only an activity in itself but a model for working and looking at ourselves as well as our group.

1. Show the gathering what the activity is designed to do. Don't hide any part of the agenda.
2. Divide into small groups (four people in each) and answer the following questions:
   A. What do you see as the major strengths of this church, group, or committee?
   B. What do you see as obstacles (in self, group, and institution), preventing us from using our strengths to the fullest?
3. Have the small groups report back their conclusions larger assembly.
   A. Focus on weakness only as they relate to strengths. In this way avoid centering on complaints, gripes, and other negative responses.
   B. What specific steps could be taken to begin to maximize our strengths and correct our weaknesses?
4. At this point—either in plenary session or in small groups, depending on size—move on to consensus building, theological reflection, common direction, definition of next steps, responsibilities, resources needed, and target dates. (It is essential to move to some decision making in this process. Too many of us have been asked what we feel and have had our information recorded, filed, and shelved. The purpose of self-assessment is not only to gather valid information but also to enable a group to move with that data to some positive outcome.)

Beliefs and Rituals

The vision of an organization may be best understood through an assessment of the myths and rituals which lie at the roots of its corporate life. Harrison Owen, in his contribution to *Transforming Work* (Adams, 209ff.), describes myths and rituals as the critical mechanisms that provide drive and excitement in an organization's culture. The term *belief* may be a helpful synonym for the word *myth* in this discussion.

Beliefs and rituals reveal much about issues, events, problems, people, and words with particular meanings. The significance of a choice of word, for example, is revealed in the experience of St. Andrew Presbyterian Church of Albuquerque, New Mexico. The charter members chose not to be called St. Andrew's Presbyterian Church, feeling that the possessive should not be applied since the congregation was being named for him.

Members do not belong to the original St. Andrew. Newer members not present on the day of naming can recite the story of why there is no apostrophe and s at St. Andrew. The meaning of names and events is powerful. Facts are not necessarily important in such stories, since the underlying beliefs carry independent import. To know and understand the history/stories of an organization is to know and understand much that is the root of the group's corporate life.

Rituals are the dramatic reenactment of beliefs and central stories. Original events are again experienced. Unique celebrations emerge, which carry meanings that are important to the congregation. Each church develops special ways of celebrating what is at the heart of its life. For example, most church communities have some unique event, held each year, with roots in the life of that particular membership. It may be a bazaar, a pancake breakfast, a holiday potluck meal, a celebration of a long-ago fire, a seder, a summer social, a homecoming, an Easter vigil, an educational event, or a mission fair. By discovering that ritual event and assessing its meaning, much may be revealed about what that group believes. Congregations tend to ritualize their stories.

Beliefs and rituals can provide an effective source for descriptive self-assessment. The following process may be helpful in assisting a group to describe what they do, discuss, and believe, and thus promote discussion that will heighten awareness of their life together.

Identifying Beliefs and Rituals

In order to discover some of our basic beliefs, it may be helpful to think about and describe aspects of some of our congregation's important stories and activities. Use the following worksheet to reflect upon them. In the accounts, who or what are important:

> Issues   —
> Events   —
> Problems —
> People   —
> Words   —

In a group, discuss what you have discovered. What beliefs seem to lie at the root of the life of your community? Are some dominant? Are they so powerfully held that others are ignored or limited in their impact on the ministry and mission of the church? Are the rituals of our community in concert with our beliefs? What issues, concerns, or points of celebration revealed by this conversation might warrant further attention? What is the impact of the dominant beliefs on people and groups? Are any segments of the congregation restive because of the limits imposed by some of these beliefs?

Prescriptive Self-Assessment

In the previous chapter, prescriptive self-assessment was defined as an appraisal of an organization or some aspect of its life. This type of assessment assumes some theological perspective, or understanding of ministry and mission. It creates an idea or word-picture of what the congregation should be doing, believing, or thinking. Thus it creates norms against which the organization may be evaluated. The following pages present several prescriptive instruments.

How It Feels Here

Leaders detect much apathy among members and therefore they create an instrument that enables those involved to assess the spirit or climate of the congregation and suggest ways in which this atmosphere can be improved.

The Climate of the Church Organization

We are interested in the overall climate of this congregation. While this is not a tangible thing, there is usually pretty good agreement as to what the general climate is and what it feels like at any given time.The main point is this: How does it feel when you attend worship or work with others in task groups and committees?

Below, please give us your feelings about the climate by placing a check in the appropriate space. For example:

		X						
Fearful	1	2	3	4	5	6	7	Not Fearful

This would show you that the congregational milieu is quite intimidating. A check toward the right-hand side would show that you felt the atmosphere was less threatening; a check in the middle would suggest that either you experience your surroundings as neutral or you cannot say distinctly what you feel.

Do this for each pair of words or phrases below. Don't worry about whether you are accurate; give your best estimate of the "feel" of this congregation. Work quickly.

1. Alert	1	2	3	4	5	6	7	Not Alert
2 Trustful	1	2	3	4	5	6	7	Mistrustful
3. Cooperative	1	2	3	4	5	6	7	Uncooperative

4. Supportive	1	2	3	4	5	6	7	Unsupportive
5. Personal and close	1	2	3	4	5	6	7	Impersonal and distant
6. Creative	1	2	3	4	5	6	7	Uncreative
7. Sensitive	1	2	3	4	5	6	7	Insensitive
8. Facing problems	1	2	3	4	5	6	7	Avoiding problems
9. Conservative	1	2	3	4	5	6	7	Innovative
10. Unconcerned	1	2	3	4	5	6	7	Concerned
11. Listening	1	2	3	4	5	6	7	Not listening
12. Decisions from above	1	2	3	4	5	6	7	Shared decisions
13. Rigid	1	2	3	4	5	6	7	Flexible
14. Feelings ignored	1	2	3	4	5	6	7	Feelings count
15. Divided	1	2	3	4	5	6	7	Unified
16. Relaxed	1	2	3	4	5	6	7	Tense

Task Group or Committee Effectiveness

A committee or task group is meeting infrequently and does not report on its assignments. Very few members attend meetings. Leaders create an instrument for these bodies, enabling them to assess their own effectiveness and make any needed changes.

Task Group or Committee Effectiveness

1. This task group has specific goals.

Satisfied   1   2   3   4   5   6   7   Not satisfied

2. The goals are feasible for this group to tackle.

Satisfied   1   2   3   4   5   6   7   Not satisfied

3. There is agreement about the goals of this group.

Satisfied   1   2   3   4   5   6   7   Not satisfied

4. The goals of this group are worth my time.

Satisfied   1   2   3   4   5   6   7   Not satisfied

5. My function is accepted by the group.

Satisfied   1   2   3   4   5   6   7   Not satisfied

6. I am satisfied with the way this group is doing its work.

Satisfied   1   2   3   4   5   6   7   Not satisfied

Worship Perceptions

Worship services are the subject of controversy. Leaders create an instrument that enables the membership to record their thoughts about the service and to suggest changes that might provide more meaningful worship for the total congregation.

My Perceptions of Our Worship Service

I think that:

1. The worship service reflects the desires of the total congregation.

| Agree | 1 | 2 | 3 | 4 | 5 | 6 | 7 | Disagree |

2. The worship service is regularly evaluated.

| Agree | 1 | 2 | 3 | 4 | 5 | 6 | 7 | Disagree |

3. The worship service provides the kind of congregational participation I want.

| Agree | 1 | 2 | 3 | 4 | 5 | 6 | 7 | Disagree |

4. There is flexibility and adaptability in the worship service.

| Agree | 1 | 2 | 3 | 4 | 5 | 6 | 7 | Disagree |

5. The hymns we sing reflect the preferences of the congregation.

| Agree | 1 | 2 | 3 | 4 | 5 | 6 | 7 | Disagree |

6. The congregation has a sense of expectancy and anticipation in worship.

| Agree | 1 | 2 | 3 | 4 | 5 | 6 | 7 | Disagree |

7. The sermon helps me worship.

| Agree | 1 | 2 | 3 | 4 | 5 | 6 | 7 | Disagree |

8. There are elements in the worship service that need to be changed.

| Agree | 1 | 2 | 3 | 4 | 5 | 6 | 7 | Disagree |

9. The length of the worship service is satisfactory.

| Agree | 1 | 2 | 3 | 4 | 5 | 6 | 7 | Disagree |

10. Change in the worship service upsets me.

| Agree | 1 | 2 | 3 | 4 | 5 | 6 | 7 | Disagree |

Mission in This Community

Members express concern about the involvement of the congregation in community life. Leaders create an instrument that will enable the members to see the different ways the church ought to be related to society, and then suggest ways in which these ideas can be put into practice with maximum congregational participation and enthusiasm.

The Mission of the Church in This Community

I believe that:

1. One of the major responsibilities of the church is to minister to the physical—as well as the spiritual—needs of people.

Agree	1	2	3	4	5	6	7	Disagree

2. This church has clearly defined goals for ministry to people in the community.

Agree	1	2	3	4	5	6	7	Disagree

3. This church is now as active in ministering to the needs of people in the community as I would like it to be.

Agree	1	2	3	4	5	6	7	Disagree

4. The church has an obligation to help its members minister to others in everyday life.

Agree	1	2	3	4	5	6	7	Disagree

5. Participating in the life of this church significantly helps me fulfill my Christian responsibilities in everyday life.

Agree	1	2	3	4	5	6	7	Disagree

6. The church ought not get involved in controversial social issues.

Agree	1	2	3	4	5	6	7	Disagree

7. I feel free to express to others in this church my views on controversial social issues, even though I know many persons disagree with me.

Agree	1	2	3	4	5	6	7	Disagree

8. The pastor ought not take stands on issues when he or she knows many think differently.

Agree	1	2	3	4	5	6	7	Disagree

9. This church provides me ample opportunity for working with others in ministering to people in the community.

Agree	1	2	3	4	5	6	7	Disagree

Training Assessment

Leaders suspect that there has not been adequate training of task groups and committees. Important programs have not been implemented or the reporting of congregational goals has been delayed. An instrument is created to identify or suggest training needs and to evaluate the effectiveness of previous training.

Assessment of Task Group or Committee Training

1. Three important tasks of this committee are:
   a.

   b.

   c.

2. This committee has clearly defined each task.

Agree	1	2	3	4	5	6	7	Disagree

3. We are organized to achieve each task.

Agree	1	2	3	4	5	6	7	Disagree

4. We make good use of our time as a committee.

Agree	1	2	3	4	5	6	7	Disagree

5. All members feel free to express themselves, even to the point of standing alone.

Agree	1	2	3	4	5	6	7	Disagree

6. Members value others' contributions.

Agree	1	2	3	4	5	6	7	Disagree

7. This committee is now as active in fulfilling its task as I would like it to be.

Agree	1	2	3	4	5	6	7	Disagree

8. Participating in this committee significantly helps me fulfill my Christian responsibility in everyday life.

Agree	1	2	3	4	5	6	7	Disagree

Congregational Goals

The congregation has participated in a goal-setting process, but there appears to be little enthusiasm for the objectives or any commitment to them. Leaders use an instrument to enable members to examine their relationship to the goals and suggest ways in which their own enthusiasm and commitment can be increased.

Assessment of Congregational Goals

This is an instrument designed to help you indicate your understanding of the goals of this congregation. There are no right or wrong answers. Check the space that best expresses your perception about the goals.

1. The goals of this congregation are clear to me.

Agree	1	2	3	4	5	6	7	Disagree

2. The goals of this congregation are implicit.

Agree	1	2	3	4	5	6	7	Disagree

3. Someone else has established the goals of this congregation.

Agree	1	2	3	4	5	6	7	Disagree

4. My personal goals are consistent with the goals of the congregation.

Agree	1	2	3	4	5	6	7	Disagree

5. I have been involved in establishing the goals of this congregation.

Agree	1	2	3	4	5	6	7	Disagree

6. It is clear to me how we are moving to achieve our goals.

Agree	1	2	3	4	5	6	7	Disagree

7. The goals of this congregation are unexamined.

Agree	1	2	3	4	5	6	7	Disagree

Leadership Style

Leaders feel that there are negative feelings toward them in the congregation. An instrument is designed to identify such feelings and the basis for them. Actions that leaders could take to increase their own effectiveness are explored.

Perceptions of Leadership Style

Use this instrument to help leaders of this congregation understand how you view their style, and how you think they could increase their effectiveness. On each of the items, mark an X to indicate how you perceive this congregation.

	1	2	3	4	5	6	7	
Goal-setting by pastor or key leadership								Goal-setting by congregation
Decision-making by a few people. Power in few key members.								Decision making in places where there are different perspectives on the decision.
Climate of congregation reinforces conformity and uniformity.								Climate is supportive, encourages respect for differences.
Downward communications from leadership group.								Two-way communication between leaders and others.

	1	2	3	4	5	6	7	
Hidden agendas in most meetings.	1	2	3	4	5	6	7	Freedom to express differences openly.
Leadership imposes its will on congregation.	1	2	3	4	5	6	7	Joint determination of what and how things should be done.
Authority based on roles and status.	1	2	3	4	5	6	7	Authority based on knowledge and competence.
Conflict ignored, repressed, smoothed over.	1	2	3	4	5	6	7	Conflict managed by leaders.
Status quo. Established procedures valued most highly.	1	2	3	4	5	6	7	Flexibility. Congregation able to cope with change plus search for better methods and solutions.
"Business as usual."	1	2	3	4	5	6	7	Built-in mechanisms for continuous evaluations and improvement.

How Do I Feel About Our Congregation?

During the year, leaders have heard criticisms about different facets of the congregation's life. A committee has kept a list of comments and used them to create an instrument for use at an annual meeting, so that the congregation can fully examine its life and make suggestions for improvement.

How Do I Feel About Our Congregation?

I think that:

1. The congregation regularly evaluates and reviews its mission aims, and goals.

Agree	1	2	3	4	5	6	7	Disagree

2. We have an effective program for leadership recruitment and training.

Agree	1	2	3	4	5	6	7	Disagree

3. Individuality and creativity are encouraged.

Agree	1	2	3	4	5	6	7	Disagree

4. There is a high level of motivation in the congregation.

Agree	1	2	3	4	5	6	7	Disagree

5. Communication channels are open and working.

Agree	1	2	3	4	5	6	7	Disagree

6. The congregational organization is flexible and adaptable.

Agree	1	2	3	4	5	6	7	Disagree

7. The membership includes people of varying ages, backgrounds, and interests.

Agree	1	2	3	4	5	6	7	Disagree

8. Disagreement and conflict are adequately dealt with.

Agree	1	2	3	4	5	6	7	Disagree

9. The congregation's accomplishments and shortcomings are evaluated regularly.

Agree	1	2	3	4	5	6	7	Disagree

10. Members from every level of congregational life help shape decisions through person-to-person communication.

Agree	1	2	3	4	5	6	7	Disagree

11. The congregation is able to cope with change.

Agree	1	2	3	4	5	6	7	Disagree

12. The congregation supports and encourages its members.

Agree	1	2	3	4	5	6	7	Disagree

8

A Goal-Setting Process

Goal setting through establishing mission directions or congregational purposes is a key activity in developing an active congregation. Clarity of intention is crucial in designing such a process. Most governing boards have not been specific about what they mean by authorizing goal setting. Intention should affect design in direct ways; therefore, governing boards must articulate their own understanding of the results they desire. Possible alternative outcomes are:

1. A written statement of goals and objectives for governing board action.
2. A study paper for the governing board and congregation, produced by a church "think tank" that looks at the future and gathers information. (No action is expected, and there is no plan or strategy to activate the congregation to implement the recommendations of the study.)
3. Intensive and extensive congregational involvement in developing common ministry and mission objectives, and a mutual commitment to achieving the goals.
4. The design of a congregational structure, allocation of resources, and creation of communication and decision-making processes that will enable the congregation and its committees and task groups to be effective.
5. Identification and mobilization of people and other resources to achieve goals.

Frequently governing boards think that establishing mission statements will produce a common commitment and will mobilize resources. However, there is nothing intrinsically powerful enough in written communication to activate people who are marginal, skeptical, or inactive members. There is distrust of these communiques. People are energized by human processes that encourage them to see the relationship between documents and their own passions and commitments. If goal 5 is the desired outcome, then goals 3 and 4 must also be adopted. In participating congregations, the most intensive and extensive procedures have been used, focusing on member involvement, development needed to achieve goals, and mobilization of resources. Effective achievement at each step increases the positive participation of church members.

This chapter will continue the description of suggested processes for information gathering, goal setting, and objective formation. Subsequent chapters will contain specific designs for training people to strive for goals and objectives more effectively.

It is important to recognize again that goal and objective formulation is but a first step. An effective organizational design that brings people and resources together to achieve specific tasks is crucial. Since existing committees already have goals and objectives, assigning them new ones will increase their work load and almost certainly guarantee ineffectiveness. It does not provide them with discrete tasks on which they can focus their limited resources. Training for specific achievement and good planning will further increase the possibility that committee members will be effective, remain active, and inspire the congregation to become even more successful in its ministry and mission.

There are several definitions of goal and objective. The following are used in this book.

A *goal* is a qualitative state or set of conditions that is desired at some time in the future. It is a direction to be pursued in congregational life.

An *objective* is a particular state or set of conditions in the future that is definable and measurable and will enable persons to achieve a goal or move in a desired direction. An objective may be one or more of a specific series of steps in the achievement of a goal.

Guidelines for Writing Objectives

An objective written for the congregation should meet as many of the following criteria as possible:

1. IT IS GOAL-DIRECTED. It can be clearly seen as a help toward achieving a larger goal.
2. IT IS DESIRABLE. It grows out of congregational interests and needs that have been expressed, or it represents the leader's conviction that it will promote a healthier and more effective church organization.
3. IT IS UNDERSTANDABLE. It can be expressed in words that are comprehended.
4. IT IS ASSIGNABLE. People asked to work on it can see their task clearly.

5. IT IS CONCEIVABLE. Its accomplishment can be visualized as entirely possible.
6. IT IS ACHIEVABLE. The existing resources (or those that can be secured) of time, skills, materials, facilities, and dollars are sufficient to do the task.
7. IT IS MEASURABLE. Observers can tell when it is finished, and some judgment can be made about whether it was worthwhile to do.
8. IT IS CONTROLLABLE. It produces a minimum of unintended consequences; people are not involved unintentionally or without their permission.

Goal setting is but one part of the activation process that we have designed and implemented with congregations. There are five steps in all:

First comes the creation of vision. It is the task of leaders of corporations to create a vision through which an organization may get a glimpse of the future to which God is calling it. Such a vision is inspiring and causes others to be involved when it is presented in a public fashion. It is also full of direction while at the same time it is flexible enough to encourage the participation of a large number of people. The vision statement that follows is such an example. It was developed during a weekend officer retreat by the session and board of deacons of a Presbyterian church. It is important to note that it is full of publicly shared goals developed by leaders for themselves and opens the door for the creation of congregational goals. These wise leaders did not make the mistake of trying to detail programmatic ends for other people to accomplish.

Tentative Statement of Vision Prepared at Officers' Retreat, March 9, 1986, later adopted by Session. First Presbyterian Church exists to praise and serve Jesus Christ on earth and to glorify God. We want to be a church characterized as sensitive, caring, responsive, courageous, loving, 'on fire', warm, open and forgiving. We are dedicated people living our Christian beliefs.

We need to be able to effectively communicate within the congregation through a system that recognizes and enhances the abilities and talents of individual members. We recognize the need to be organized in a manner that facilitates decision making, but at the same time is flexible enough to meet the changing needs of our congregation, community and world.

We are a church of Christian achievers not afraid of failure. We need to plan specific objectives and continuously evaluate every area of our church's life. In order to achieve success, the congregation, especially its officers, must be willing to make a personal commitment to become ministers ministering to our congregation, community and world.

—First Presbyterian Church, LaGrange, Illinois.

Second is an information-gathering process that seeks to elicit the concepts and commitments of as many members as possible about the mission, purposes, goals, tasks, and environmental undertakings of the congregation. The design of the process should include all members—active and inactive—in sharing information and listening to one another. There are differences that can be clarified, examined, confirmed, or disproved. Additional information, alternative perceptions, and ways to work on personal commitments can be provided in public settings.

In this stage, leaders are attempting to identify the common purposes, tasks, and challenges that can be the foundation for creating an effective, mobilized congregation. Members have to tell one another—as well as their leaders—the basis for their activation.

Some churches have established study committees prior to congregational involvement processes. These units have done exhaustive studies with very high quality work, only to discover that they are unable to mobilize the congregation around the finished product. Study committees can work well for the congregation if they only expect the church members to reflect on their creation while at the same time holding their own perceptions and commitments. It is possible for a matching to take place between aspects of the work of the committee and an individual's hopes for and concerns about the congregation.

The central purpose of this information-gathering step is to design a process in which the congregation can listen to diverse ideas about its future direction and reflect on what is heard. The goal is to take a first step toward commitment to the future.

Third, a goal-formulation and priority-development process uses the information from the congregation as the basis for a preliminary testing of its intent. Both positive and negative information can be used to develop statements of goals or purposes. A negative evaluation of some aspect of church life can be restated as a positive direction for the members, if leaders and the congregation affirm the validity of the concern and the goal that will be responsive to it.

Both confirmation of goal statements and establishment of priorities need to be intentional processes. Many people do not recognize their hopes and concerns when these are translated into formal statements. The integrity of people in processes is maintained through cycles in which they confirm that the formulation of goals and objectives expresses their intentions for the congregation and community. During these cycles, participants can look at the work of committees or task groups and see that their work reflects, in a satisfying way, their own understanding of the issues. These cycles are important also as educational processes for other members, who see the results in the total congregation. Goal statements reflecting the wide range of interests, theological commitments, and concerns of the congregation, and resulting from an intensive human process, help to sensitize a congregation to its members and its community. This step is a valuable aspect of enlarging the concerns of members of the congregation.

Fourth, the planning and implementation processes need to begin with the identification of members with the necessary skills and interests, and the time and willingness to pursue and grapple with congregational goals. This step allows people to pledge commitment to a goal, objective, or tasks for a specific period of time.

Organizational arrangements need to be created to facilitate achievement of congregational goals. The current style of congregational work needs to be examined for effectiveness. Most churches have committees with multiple goals and objectives set in no discernible order. Traditional committees have so many tasks that they perform few of them with clarity and distinction. They act without focusing limited resources on priority needs. Most committees have a life of their own which includes habitual ways of acting, responding, developing programs, and establishing their own goals and preferences—which may or may not be responsive to the needs of the whole congregation.

Congregations will generally obtain better quality work, and members of work groups will have greater involvement and higher morale, if they are given a discrete objective to attain, with adequate resources, authority to pursue the objective, and a definite time period for their work. Committees composed of volunteers have difficulty focusing their time, energy, and resources on specific items when multiple objectives, functions and tasks are assigned to them.

A structure needs to be created that will bring people together who are committed to a particular congregational goal or objective, and who have authority to achieve the goal for the congregation. Task groups with a single focus are preferable to committees with multiple, undistinguished aims. In addition, volunteers must be trained to achieve effectively goals and objectives to which they are committed, and modest but helpful planning procedures must be developed to enable a congregation to accomplish its ends effectively. Reaching goals is important, not only to those people assigned the responsibility, but also to the congregation. The church that has established goals for itself, then carried them out well, will become increasingly active as it senses that it is doing what it said it needed and wanted to do for itself and the community.

Fifth, public evaluative efforts need to be undertaken. Actors and recipients of their activity will learn, grow, and move into a future that grows out of a healthy understanding of the past. A legitimate evaluation is produced through use of clear, agreed-upon criteria.

An activating process includes all of the above stages. The end product is a congregation in which members are mobilized, organized, and trained to achieve the goals that are important to them, individually and corporately. Active congregations are more effective in caring for themselves, for individuals in their midst, and for the communities in which they reside.

The activation process outlined in Table 2 has been followed in many congregations. A leadership group using it should make modifications to reflect their church's particular style of information gathering and way of involving the congregation in thinking about the value, worthiness, and appropriateness of the established goals.

Table 2 A Process for Activating a Congregation

Task	Action	Special Concerns
A) Appoint task group to implement the process.	The Governing board appoint a task group after clarifying its leadership vision.	Design the task group to include the various interests of the congregation. Include specific authorization for the task, including the objectives of the particular group.
B) The task group develops a clear understanding of its assignments.	Organize the task group to achieve its aim, including data gathering, goal and objective formulation, organizational training, and planning tasks.	Clarify the authorization and objectives of the governing board in appointing group. (See outcomes listed at the opening of this chapter. Note particularly the last three in light of authorization by the governing board.)
C) The task group organizes an information-gathering process.	Create a design for gathering information. Train group leaders and organize meetings. (See Agenda for Home Meetings in the Appendix.)	The process should reach as many members of the congregation as possible. Special attention should be given to inactive members. Meetings may be conducted in homes of inactive members to ensure their involvement. (See Additional Ways of Gathering Information in the Appendix.)

Task	Action	Special Concerns
D) The task group gathers information.	Trained leaders meet with small groups to gather information to be used in forming the goals and objectives of the congregation.	(See Special Problems in Gathering Information in the Appendix.)
E) The task group formulates goals and objectives.	Task group meets with leaders of small groups to develop tentative statements.	(A design for this process is suggested in Steps in Goal and Objective Formation in the Appendix.)
F) The task group submits goals and objectives to the governing board.	Review, revise, or create a method for presentation to the congregation with recommendations that will enable the congregation to reflect on the quality of its goals.	Reflecting as Christians about Congregational Goals (in the Appendix) discusses methods for facilitating congregational reflection. The task of the governing board is to help the congregation assess the quality of the vision it has created for itself.
G) The governing board submits priority goals, objectives, and recommendations to the congregation for action.	The congregation reviews, revises, discusses, reflects upon, and develops priorities among recommendations of the task group and governing board.	The governing board may submit an organizational design for achieving the primary goals and objectives. This is an occasion when persons should be encouraged to volunteer to work on specific priority goals and objectives.

(Continued on following page)

Task	Action	Special Concerns
H) The governing board creates an organizational design.	Determine style of the organization. Name task groups to achieve specific goals or objectives depending upon the group and the number of objectives to be met. Assign persons who have volunteered to work on a specific goal or objective. Choose chairpersons who can develop effective working groups and who have a strong desire to see that the group achieves its goal. As each group is appointed, a budget should be provided along with authorization to meet the goal and its designated objectives. Reporting procedures and times should be indicated, and the date for evaluation of the group's work by a committee of the cong-regation should be established.	As task groups are appointed, plans for training should be made and shared with members.
I) The governing board provides training to help each task group effectively plan its goals and objectives.	Appoint a committee to design and implement ways to train task groups in gaining goals and objectives.	(See Chapters 10, 11, and 12 for discussions and designs for training and planning for effectiveness.)

Task	Action	Special Concerns
J) The governing board establishes date for evaluation of each task group as a basis of the next cycle of goal setting.	Appoint an evaluation committee. Establish a schedule for critiquing the work of various task groups.	(See Chapter 13 for a discussion of the evaluation.)

9

Prioritization

Church organizations can become incapacitated by committing themselves to too many goals. Churches can be at one moment very active, then suddenly—and surprisingly—become full of passive members. Such passivity is likely if churchgoers have not experienced their activity as leading to the fulfillment of personal, group, or congregational goals. In other words, passivity can be the outcome if high levels of activity seem to lead nowhere. If goals are unrealistically cast, people will become frustrated trying to accomplish them. There are limits to the number of commitments an active organization can pursue. Therefore, it is important that active churches be selective about what they attempt.

We live in a post-modern era, where humankind possesses both the technology and the resources to accomplish more than it may wish. For example, researchers and designers are capable of inventing more types and greater numbers of weapons than nations may want. The capacity of medical technology to stretch the bounds of death also raises the issue of selectivity. Many people find no value in prolonging life under certain conditions. Thus, in the post-modern era, we face a need to develop processes that help people decide what can and cannot be accomplished. The capacity to conceptualize and to accomplish does not, by itself, connote implementation. There remains the problem of choice.

The activation processes described in this book are likely to give rise to more goals than can be reasonably implemented. Therefore, it may become necessary to choose among goals that differ in desirability, appropriateness, and timeliness. If leaders fail to assist groups in making realistic choices, problems will result. If a congregation with limited resources commits itself to multiple goals, when it can only succeed with a limited number, it will find itself spread so thin that it will become frustrated and accomplish little. Wise leaders must enable individuals to commit themselves to levels of activity that stretch them without thwarting their enthusiasm.

Numerous techniques can assist groups in making choices. A simple forced-choice process can be easily designed. This approach compels either individuals or small groups to select a limited number of possible objectives. Casting votes for a few among many options provides training for later decision making. For example, each leader on a governing board might be invited to vote for three top choices among eight possibilities. As with most instruments, such a process is not meant to be statistically determinative but to provide insight for conversations within which real decisions are made. At its best, such communication enables various leaders to understand and value the life and interdependence of the organization's subunits. However, such a procedure often ranks excellent ideas as mediocre. It is wise to retain such "extra" ideas for future evaluation; they should not be forgotten. If implementation of high priorities goes well, it may be possible to approve other choices.

The design of a particular process for evaluating assorted commitments is not very significant, but it is important that leaders help organizations take upon themselves challenges which do not frustrate their enthusiasm. Attractively printed statements of goals have no value if they collect dust on the top shelves of church offices or take up space in filing cabinets. Unachievable goals result from commitment making that fails to assess correctly present and future realities. To achieve a series of doable—yet ever more challenging and faithful—goals is a far better vision than is an inappropriate attempt to usher in the reign of God.

10

Planning for Doing

Commitment making, as described in the previous chapters, should not be attempted without the accompanying determination to engage in implementation processes. There can be no effective planning without goals. The setting of goals as a link between commitment and implementation is necessary in both simple and complex organizations. Planning is the means to insure that goal setting is not an empty exercise. Serious problems can emerge when goal setting and planning are absent from the work of committees, congregations, and denominations. Participants frequently feel frustrated when decisions—publicly made—are never pursued. It is disastrous to engage in public decision-making processes that go nowhere. Failing to link commitment and implementation is a common mistake made by revitalization theoreticians and practitioners. This fault can be avoided either by not making empty resolutions or, preferably, by planning for both commitment and implementation as a unit.

Planning

During the past fifteen years, denominations have placed an increasing emphasis on planning processes. Declining resources, uncertainty as to the best response to different environmental challenges, and diversity of goals required for the different populations of denominations have all required specialized planning. However, very few congregations and judicatories have actually done it. Denominations have met with mixed success in planning. Several that began preparation at the national level have met with dismal failure and have encountered much hostility to their efforts.

The theory of activation developed in this book implies systematic planning that will increase the effectiveness of volunteers who possess increasingly limited time and energy. Planning enables churches to organize tasks, time, resources, and people with increased effectiveness.

Planning has met resistance when it has not been helpful to church members. This has occurred primarily because of the complexity of most planning processes used in the church. When complex industrial or military planning methods have been adopted, they have not been perceived as helpful. Pastors have not been educated to think systematically and use these processes, while volunteer members do not have the time or energy for them. A method is needed that is simple, direct, and readily learned so that volunteers can use it effectively and see accurately what is involved in achieving an objective.

Planning by volunteers needs to be a public proceeding, one in which the members who must implement also develop the plans. In such a process members have a more precise understanding of the task, the resources needed, and how much time a particular task will take. They then know what is expected of them and can be held accountable for doing it.

Too frequently groups have only a vague idea of what they are after if they have not used a goal-setting process to clarify their objective. Consequently, no one can be held accountable or responsible for anything. Morale declines, and nothing happens.

The First Step: Clarity About Direction

Often church members begin to pursue a particular goal armed with sufficient energy and time, but as endless meetings follow in which no progress is made, they become discouraged. Task groups begin with a general direction but often do not know how to take that first important step.

Effective planning begins with a statement of an objective to be reached. A simple sentence stating what needs to be accomplished by a particular date is crucial.

Example 1. A plan for recruiting new members will be designed by September 1.

Example 2. A new curriculum for senior high young people will have been taught for one quarter in the fall, and an evaluation of the curriculum will have been made by the Curriculum Subcommittee of the Church Education Committee by March 30.

The Second Step: Identifying the End Product

Rarely do committees or task groups pause deliberately and ask: How would the successful achievement of the objective look? This is an important question to ask if effectiveness is to be increased. Answering the question involves specifying programs, people, resources, money, and facilities that will actually exist when the objective is reached. Example 2 (above) exemplifies this point:

> A new curriculum for senior high young people will have been selected.
> Teachers will have been recruited and trained.

·   A specific amount of money for purchase of curriculum will have been provided.

A senior high class will have used the curriculum for one quarter.

The Curriculum Subcommittee will have designed and administered an evaluation of the class.

The Curriculum Subcommittee will have reported the results of its evaluation to the Church Education Committee by March 30.

If members cannot imagine at least some of what should be present when their objectives are reached, the group is going nowhere. If a direction and some end products cannot be specified within an established period of time, then either the committee should be disbanded and a new group formed, or the original objective should be reviewed, revised, or dropped as a realistic objective of the congregation.

When a listing has been made of conditions that will be present if the objective is met, then the committee and the governing board have additional knowledge with which to work. From such a listing a catalogue of tasks to be done, money and resources needed, and the kinds of people necessary can be compiled. The committee has a concrete way of evaluating whether it has the personnel, resources, and time to achieve its aim. There can be candor and intentionality in assessing the prospect of achieving the desired end. The group may say, We do not have the resources and cannot imagine ourselves accomplishing the task, or it may declare, We can do it, but we need three more members who have the following skills. . . . They may turn to the governing board: The budgeted money is insufficient; we need more. Here is documentation of what we must have.

The Third Step: Developing a Plan

When a committee has clearly specified the conditions necessary for their objective to be met, it is ready to develop a simple plan.

The Worksheet for Planning Who, What and When provides the framework for developing such a plan. The key elements include: *what*—the tasks that need to be done to ensure that the identified conditions will be present; *who*—the names of people needed to do the work; and *when*—the designated time for performing the tasks. The plan should be developed by the committee, and at that time people present should volunteer to take on a specific job.

As tasks, people, and time are identified, money, facilities and other resources should also be listed. This provides the basis for developing a budget. Planning enables leaders and congregations to know the needs of groups and to allocate the available resources. Accurate budgeting is impossible without planning. The type of money arrangements suggested in this chapter equips governing boards and congregations to know what resources are needed, to identify resources available, and then to search for whatever additional resources are necessary.

Planning also provides a valid basis for stewardship programs. A governing board is able to assess the needs of the congregation and then challenge members to give time, energy, money, and other resources in order to reach their own priority goals and objectives. Stewardship supports the plans of the congregation to do what they have said is important. Planning, budgeting, and stewardship of resources are integral activities in activating congregations.

Most congregations develop their budgets by adding to, or subtracting from the previous year's spending, some by as much as 3, 6, or 10 percent. Budgets reflect neither the priority goals and objectives of the congregation nor its commitments and intentions. Traditional budgets do not generate the confidence or enthusiasm of members. Many support such budgets out of a sense of duty, not out of conviction that the congregation is clear about its directions, has plans to be effective, and knows the needed resources. Much of traditional budgeting rests on the trust of leaders and the goodwill of members. When either trust diminishes or goodwill declines—or when both occur—then budgeting and stewardship programs fail.

Three simple processes of planning have been used in congregations. Formats for these are provided in the following worksheets. The major concern is to use a process that has a simple and workable format. The process itself is not the central focus of planning, but it is instrumental in enabling a congregation to formulate simple, workable plans. Leaders should modify whatever they think will work for them. It is important not to get bogged down in the process of planning and thereby diminish the enthusiasm and the effectiveness of volunteers.

Worksheet for Planning Who, What, When

1. State the objective to be achieved.

2. Identify everything which would be present to successfully complete the objective, that is, the number of people, the amount of supplies and money, and the type of facilities needed.

3. Complete the following planning sheet, identifying what needs to happen, by whom, and at what time in order for the objectives to be achieved.

A. Specific amount of time needed before events or decisions take place in days, weeks, months, or years.

B. Specific tasks for meeting objective, include what needs to be done at designated times?

C. Volunteers who will do specific tasks at designated times.

D. Resources needed for task at each designated time, that is, supplies, facilities, materials, and so on.

E. Estimated amount of money needed for resources at each designated time.

Worksheet for Time Planning to Identify Resources

1. State the objective.
2. Complete the worksheet by identifying the resources needed during each time period.

Time When Resources Are Needed							
Time Period:	1	2	3	4	5	6	7 . . .
1. People: How many volunteers and what skills should they have?							
2. Time: How much time is needed to accomplish each task?							
3. Money: How much is needed during each time period?							
4. Facilities and materials: What resources are needed at each time interval?							

Worksheet for Planning Steps to Accomplish Objectives

Objective:	1.	2.	3.

Identify what we
hope to accomplish

What will results
look like if we
achieve objective?

What needs to be
done? (specific
steps)

Who will do it
and when?

Resources needed?

Who will evaluate
and when?

11

The Support and Training of Volunteers

Much of the planning strategy discussed in the previous chapter relates to the use of church members. All of God's people have been given gifts meant to be used—but not wasted. To help faithful people discern, develop, and use their gifts in fulfilling ways is an act of public beneficence by leaders. Members and leaders are mutually responsible for their common life in public witness and service. A necessary calling for church leaders is the support of broad and deep development of God-given gifts among all members.

The health of any church body is unlikely to be greater than that of the organizations within it. Careful nurture of subunits is, therefore, critically important for leaders. The style of the leader core is likely to be mirrored in the entire church, for better or for worse. A conscious strategy of modeling healthful leadership styles and the development of new leadership is essential. If active leaders deal only with one another, their numbers dwindle. The future must include resourceful people, prepared to pursue the corporate vision.

Training for Effectiveness

Little research has been done on the effectiveness of various methods of training. Consequently, there is no way of knowing the worth of such procedures. The church has spent millions of dollars instructing teachers, church officers, youth advisers, stewardship committees, and others. Middle-level organizations, such as presbyteries, synods, dioceses, and conferences, have usually provided the resources and personnel for training. Frequently the content and design serve to meet the goals, needs, and abilities of the denomination and/or middle judicatory personnel, rather than those of particular churches. Often they are imposed on other congregations, regardless of their unique contexts, sizes, and circumstances.

Such imposition is almost never intentional, even though there are denominational representatives who believe they know best for certain congregations. More often staff are enthusiastic about what has worked for them, or they desire to be helpful but are limited by their own learning and experiences to those training programs in which they are or have been involved.

Church officer training has also been narrowly conceived by several denominations as training in doctrine and law. Learning the content of church polity has been emphasized, as though use of historically developed procedures and belief in a particular doctrinal position should be the primary characteristics of church leaders. Even this training has not been evaluated for its effectiveness. There is no evidence that training in ecclesiastical law and doctrine has affected the use of that law or the beliefs of church officers. There is certainly no evidence that such training has had a positive impact on a congregation. No clear relationship has been shown between training and the activities of congregational leaders: the link between training and effective leadership is not clear.

Training leaders needs to be related directly to what they do. The goals and objectives of congregations vary as the communities surrounding them differ. The aim of leaders is to maintain a congregation that is effective in ministry and mission in its community. Training should enable them to develop and sustain such a ministry. The teaching of correct doctrine and church law must have a direct relation to such a goal.

Traditional training of officers appears to isolate them from the congregation and community. Effective training will help leaders to motivate committees to move toward specific goals and objectives in relation to the dynamic and changing needs of the community. Programs are justified when they actually equip leaders to do their jobs while working with others. Generalized training has limited usefulness because most congregational leaders do not know how to apply these programs to the specific problems of congregations. Most share information rather than train people. Sharing new resources, programs, and procedures must be placed in the context of other training programs at the congregational level. In this way an integration takes place that includes goals and objectives, tasks necessary to achieve these, and the utilization of resources.

Activation of members depends upon training designed to equip them to honor their commitments and to become increasingly effective in the limited time available. Training must deal with planning and then with equipping people to do what they have planned. They should learn to identify tasks, the order in which they need to be performed, and the resources needed to do them. In addition trainees should learn how to bring these critical elements together.

A Design for Effective Training

An effective training design used in working with congregations has the following elements:

1. *A clear definition of what the group (church officers, committee, or task group) must do to achieve its objectives.* Tasks should be defined as clearly as possible. People who are performing the tasks should see the relation of their tasks to the objective and to the goal that objective is helping to achieve. Members need to see how what they are doing fits into the whole of congregational life and that their activity is worth while. Job descriptions are frequently appropriate for individuals and groups.

2. *The identification of resources needed to do the task.* Resources include people, ideas, skills, tools, programs, curricula, methods, facilities, and money. People may have a clear understanding of a task without knowing what resources they will need to complete it. One aspect of resource identification is choosing among alternatives, which may mean that the committee or task group must develop criteria for the selection of necessary materials.

Recall from the previous chapter the example objective—to identify a curriculum for senior highs, teach the curriculum during the fall quarter, and evaluate the class by the following March. A task in achieving this objective is the selection of one curriculum from among numerous resources for this age group. These resources need to be examined and one—or a combination of several—selected. What criteria are to be used in examining and selecting the curriculum?

A training session may be needed for the selecting group so that they can develop a list of criteria to use in examining various curricula and in making a final selection. First, the task group will need to know what the congregation desires to share of its understanding of Christian faith, and how it wants to share it. The group would then attempt to identify areas of the faith that their youth are seeking to understand and experience. They must then identify which forms and style of interaction that would be most beneficial.

The task is then to check available resources against the criteria. The task group now has a basis for deciding which curricula are the best ones for the church's youth.

3. *A plan to schedule tasks and secure resources as needed to achieve the objective.* Groups may know what the objective is, understand the tasks needed to achieve the objective, and have the resources, but they may not know how to put objective, tasks, and resources together systematically. Developing a workable plan is an important aspect of training. Doing so increases the chances that committees and task groups will be effective. Having a plan that indicates the next steps to be taken increases the prospects that the procedure will be followed (see chapter 10 for more

about planning). Most training programs inspire groups but do not leave them with concrete ways to proceed when the training is concluded.

A plan for proceeding provides members of task groups and committees with public knowledge of what is expected of them. Accountability is, therefore increased.

4. *Evaluation of training done by persons being trained.* Evaluation may occur at several points in the training process. First, it is helpful to conduct an evaluation at the end of each session. Such an evaluation should be simple and direct. An evaluation using the following instrument will enable work group members and trainers to identify possible trouble areas and suggest future training needs.

Evaluation of Training

1. The task that the group is trying to accomplish is clear to me.

Agree	1	2	3	4	5	6	7	Disagree

2. The resources needed to accomplish the task have been identified.

Agree	1	2	3	4	5	6	7	Disagree

3. We have the resources needed to be effective.

Agree	1	2	3	4	5	6	7	Disagree

4. We have a plan and know the steps we will follow in achieving the task.

Agree	1	2	3	4	5	6	7	Disagree

5. Members of this group are working together to achieve the task.

Agree	1	2	3	4	5	6	7	Disagree

Second, evaluation may be done during achievement of the task to discern if satisfactory progress is being made and to identify any unforeseen difficulties.

In-Process Evaluation

1. We are making satisfactory progress in achieving the objective.

Agree	1	2	3	4	5	6	7	Disagree

2. There are tasks for which we need training.

Agree	1	2	3	4	5	6	7	Disagree

3. Additional resources (persons, energy, skills, tools, ideas, time, money, and equipment) are needed to achieve the objective.

Agree	1	2	3	4	5	6	7	Disagree

4. We are working together to achieve the objective.

Agree	1	2	3	4	5	6	7	Disagree

5. List ways in which the group could work together more effectively:

Evaluation during implementation will enable both leaders and members of a work group to assess their own perception of progress and to identify additional training needs.

The purpose of training members of work units is to empower them, thus equipping them to work more effectively at tasks important to the congregation and to themselves. Evaluation of training lets leaders assess whether empowerment has taken place. Further theory and tools for evaluation are found in chapter 13.

12

Organizing Resources to Meet Goals

Chapter 10 describes planning processes that use a number of different resources. Chapter 11 then focuses on ways in which personnel are supported and trained. The present chapter will discuss the use of resources other than people, thus making explicit an important distinction. Ideas, facilities, time to accomplish tasks, space, methods, and money are examples of resources that need to be identified. Too frequently organizations in general, and church organizations in particular, try to implement change or solve problems through personnel shifts alone. Pastors move or are moved, workers are fired, and chairpersons are replaced. Lives are often torn apart in these transitions. However, other alternatives are frequently more appropriate.

Theory about organization has had two major streams. One is the "human relations school." This theory tends, in general terms, to look first at people and their interrelationships when they try to understand or change an organization. The other stream may be referred to as the "bureaucratic school." In this theory, resources other than people are assessed and altered, as a way of improving the organization. This simple description of the distinctions between streams provides the groundwork for a very important point. Whenever a vision needs to be pursued or a problem needs to be solved, it may be wise to look first at the impact of the use of resources such as money, space, supplies, and at the structural form through which the organization operates. Alterations in such areas may well open the window to the desired vision. Effective use of resources may be much more fulfilling than the kinds of frustrations that result from moving a variety of good people through impossible positions—and then branding them all as incompetent.

The ways in which dollars are budgeted or allocated exhibits much about the actual values of a church. Church representatives may speak dramatically, but where dollars go exposes their real values. If youth ministry, mission causes, or evangelism are presented as high priorities, but little is budgeted for them, a lack of alignment is revealed. A good linkage between implementation and assessment (as described in chapter 7) can be made by designing a process in which people use a budget to assess the life of an organization.

An additional misperception about money causes unnecessary conflict in many organizations. In the absence of clear goals, budgets are built around large items such as staff salary and building expenses. It is unwise, unfair, and inaccurate for congregations to think only that the bulk of their money goes for staff salaries, plus bricks and mortar. These should not be the goals of the church. They are merely tools of ministry. Budgets should be based upon cost-centering processes that help members to see staff and building as resources, much like utilities, stationery, telephone, and communion elements. Some portion of the cost of each of these resources, including staff salary, should be assigned among the goals of the organization. In this manner, the bulk of a congregation's budget is built around large items such as worship, education, and community service. Such a view may reveal the good news that a congregation applies most of its resources to worship of God, mission to the neighborhood, and Christian education. Members will feel gratified that the pastor and building are being well used in the attainment of the goals.

Before changing staff, it would be worthwhile to discover whether changes in the allocation of expenditures might bring about a healthier organization. Distribution of space and supplies may call for a similar reexamination. If youth ministry is a high priority, but no room and useful tools are set aside for young people is such a ministry really at the top of the list? What clues about organizational values might be revealed in an assessment of the ways in which space and supplies are allocated? It is likely that alterations in these areas could be healthy.

The structural forms around which church bodies live are like human skeletons. If the spine is bent, a limb broken, or a bone overworked, the entire body suffers. Similarly, if a suborganization is stymied in its work, a group is detached, or too few people carry out too much responsibility, the church body suffers. In many instances, solutions such as getting rid of chairpersons and firing pastors are no more helpful to congregations than is firing a doctor to cure a broken bone. In many cases, hope can be introduced or conflicts reduced through the implementation of appropriate structural alterations. Shifting the ways in which groups and individuals cooperatively carry out their mission may be the most effective route to implementing unaccomplished goals and objectives.

These three chapters on implementation (10, 11, and 12) are built upon the material that deals with the making of commitments. There is a dynamic relationship among commitments, personnel, and resource allocation. If there are significant changes in any one of these categories, that action will trigger change in each of the others. Conversely, if change is desired in one of those areas, but not provided for in the others, frustration will result. If a congregation plans, provides resources, and recruits leadership for a vacation Bible school but discovers that the person in charge is moving, the personnel shift triggers changes in the shape of the commitment and the need for resources. From the opposite direction, we observe that if a congregation wishes to engage in increased levels of evangelism but develops neither people nor resources to engage in that ministry, the goal is unlikely to be achieved. The most effective way to begin constructive change is through healthy commitment making. Once the commitments are clear, then sound staffing and resource application can result. If commitments are unclear, directions are too frequently set by individuals with strong personal goals, unfocused restructuring processes, or maintenance of past patterns of allocating resources, thus limiting resources for new directions for the congregation. These uncoordinated change processes tend to inhibit purposeful growth.

13

Evaluation: An Activity of Faithfulness

When a congregation is committed to Jesus Christ and intends to express that commitment through its corporate life, evaluation of its life is a critical process. Evaluation expresses loyalty and trust in God and provides a way to discern whether the congregation is, in fact, faithful. Viewed this way, evaluation may promote coherence among commitments, intentions, and life as experienced in the congregation. This positive understanding of evaluation suggests that it is a tool, a means, for enhancing and promoting the quality of congregational life. Evaluation—in contrast to self-assessment—depends upon clear public statements of goals as a precondition. It is always a means for checking to see if expected outcomes are present, or obtainable.

Problems arise when evaluative processes unfold in ways that are hidden from those most involved and are conducted in relationship to unclear criteria. Evaluation is unjust when it is conducted in secret. It is essential that evaluations be visible and participatory and that there be clear agreement on the standards to be used. Review should be accomplished in a cooperative manner by both those who act and those who are the recipients of the action. Those who give and receive in a program or in a task position should all be involved. Any instruments employed and any thoughts about conclusions should be publicly offered in order that further reflection, growth, and action may follow. Instruments or written conclusions are only helpful if they can be used to promote healthy behavior in people desiring to change.

The congregation with its programs, services, and activities is an instrument through which God reigns in the world. The ministry of people in the church serves to effect God's reigning. Programs, activities, and processes are therefore not ends in themselves, just as the church is not an end in itself. All human effort is in the service of God. Evaluation is one of the ways the people assess their own efforts as servants.

Evaluation, then, is a tool that helps people make moral judgments about their own lives as Christians. Personal assessment makes it possible for a congregation to examine the relationship between its existence and its faith as expressed in its symbols—such as reconciliation, grace, covenant community, justice, and love. This means that human experience can be held up and tested against the symbols and meanings of faith. Evaluation is a tool for doing practical theology.

Through evaluation, congregations may examine the relationship between their theological statements in confessions, articles of faith, and constitutions and their congregational behavior. Congregations, not just leaders, may share in determining whether their programs, liturgy, activities, and relationships match the vision, mission, understanding of ministry, and the goals of the congregation. A congregation may inquire: Do the results of our efforts express our self-understanding as a people of God?

Evaluation gives a congregation a capacity to be critical about its own life. Discourse and discernment about the relation between Christian faith and life are made possible through this means. Evaluation is thus a hopeful and redemptive process.

Finally, evaluation is an activity by which a congregation may monitor the processes of exchange between God's people and the world. A congregation may ask: Are we responsive to God's call to witness and do we serve God in the world? Are we responsive and do we join with God in what God is already doing in the world? This kind of critique may give a congregation the information it needs to expose areas of passivity and avoidance, and it may also increase the possibility of greater receptivity to the call to serve the Creator.

There are three major areas of evaluation in congregational life: intentions, plans and planning, and implementation.

Intentions

Good evaluation begins by examining the intentions of church members. These are expressed as goals and objectives toward which the congregation and its leaders have committed themselves. Appropriate questions to ask at this level of evaluation are:

—Are the goals and objectives worthy?
—Do the goals and objectives express our statements of faith adequately and appropriately?
—Do the goals and objectives really express the service and ministry of Jesus?
—What is the relationship between the congregation and community as stated in the goals of the congregation?
—Is this relationship an adequate expression of the confession of faith or the articles of faith of our congregation?

—Do the goals and objectives of the congregation genuinely meet the human and spiritual needs of members of the congregation and community?

—Is adequate concern expressed for the poor and hungry?

—Are the goals and objectives desirable? Do we really want to achieve them?

Such questions encourage a congregation to examine its own self-understanding and judge whether its intentions express that self-understanding. This kind of evaluation seeks to let the symbols—reconciliation, grace, covenant community, justice, love, and the various forms of expressions of faith such as behaviors, actions, and statements of faith—do their work of affirming, judging, criticizing, and redirecting a congregation. Such evaluation should always be done in a small group setting, where six to ten people can discuss the statements of faith, and these statements can inform and challenge members. The work of each small group should be shared with others so that a congregation has a way of speaking to itself and discussing its own life. An annual meeting of the congregation or specially called congregational meetings provides the best setting and will involve the congregation in thinking as Christians. General presentations in which particular individuals dominate the discussion should be avoided. Devise processes by which the congregation can evaluate its intentions.

Plans and Planning

Congregations almost universally intend to do more than they can actually accomplish. Christian faith symbols call for more responses from congregations than most can deliver. A multiplicity of Christian values in congregations encourage these reactions. The breakdown occurs between values and their realization; between symbols and their meanings.

Congregations lack well-conceived plans—if any exist at all. Planning to do what the congregation intends is almost nonexistent. The complexity of conditions that affect the various goals of a congregation, the scarcity of time and energy of members to work on goals, the limits imposed by the ideas about ways to achieve goals, and the effects of factors such as inflation and the increase in energy expenses make it increasingly important for leaders to plan in order to be more effective. Evaluation leads to more efficient planning in the future.

In addition, evaluation of plans and planning procedures is important for increasing the impact of leaders and of the whole congregation. Questions that may be asked include:

—Is the goal and/or objective clear? Do we know where we are headed?

—Is the path to get there clear? Do we know how to get to where we desire to go?

—Is the path realistic? Can we get there on this path? Will we have the resources on time?

—Is there sufficient time of members and others to follow the path?

—Is the planning adequate to achieve the goal and objective? Have the people doing the planning identified the important elements on the path to the goal? Does the congregation actually have the people, ideas, time, desire, and money to implement the plan as it stands? Or is another plan needed that is more modest, but one that is based upon actual congregational resources?

Leadership groups that evaluate the plans and planning of work groups can be more supportive, and they can coordinate the resources of the whole congregation to increase its effectiveness when study has identified what needs to be carried out. Once directions have been established by a congregation, leaders have the crucial tasks of evaluating plans and the quality of planning so that the congregation can do what it has said to itself it would do.

Implementation

Two types of evaluation may be used as tools for assessing implementation. Both require a stated direction with a goal and objectives or a model of what an intended direction would look like if successfully implemented. The first type of evaluation, in-process, requires not only a picture, or model, of what the goal should look like, but also a path or plan to obtain the objective or create the model. The plan includes information about who takes action, when it is taken, and what resources are needed. (See the Worksheet for Planning Who, What, When in chapter 10 for a model of such a plan.) Basically this type of evaluation identifies how far a group has come on the road leading to an intended objective. When a plan is present, the key question to be answered is: Where are we in relation to the plan to be followed?

This type of evaluation helps a group see whether it is on the intended path, where it is on that path, or what happened to slow it down, stop, or divert it to an uncharted byway. At any point, people with time, energy, skills, and ideas may be added. More money or time may be required. Or the group may conclude that by following the present plan they may never achieve the goal, because neither they nor the congregation have sufficient resources. Congregations too often have committees and task groups that work on goals and directions, but who never receive word on how they are doing. In-process evaluation provides feedback at any time so that a committee can improve both its effectiveness and its morale.

In-process evaluation is provided by looking at a particular date in the plan, and asking: What tasks should be done by this date? Who should do them? What resources should be available? When that date has come, ask if the specific tasks have been done. Have the people who were responsible for doing them followed through? Are the resources available? If not, where is the work group on the plan? What factors are responsible for its lack of progress? How does the group need assistance?

Such monitoring of progress is a positive leadership activity, one that members of work groups can view as a caring ministry. Too frequently, leadership groups that coordinate resources of a congregation give tasks to others and never ask how such a group can be cared for while it does its job. In-process evaluation may create the possibility for more effective care.

The second method for assessing implementation is end-product evaluation. This requires a vision or model of how the achievement of the goal and/or objective will eventually look. For example, if the goal is revitalization of the worship life of the congregation, a model of the major features of such worship would need to be created that includes the style of participation of the congregation, contributions of the choir and organist (including a description of their relationship to the worship of the congregation), the role of pastor and other liturgical leaders, and the type of prayers. When such a model is completed, it is simple to do an end-product evaluation by asking if the congregation is participating in worship in a way imagined in our model. Are the choir and organist contributing to the worship service in the correct manner? Is the pastor leading worship as prescribed in our model? Are other lay leaders participating in the liturgy as described? Are the prayers and other elements of the revised worship included in the liturgy?

Evaluation of this type forces groups to think about where they are headed before they begin. In the illustration above, a group must think about criteria for vital worship before making a single change. This type of evaluation improves the quality of thinking about congregational life by raising both theological and practical questions.

Church groups do not normally ask, What will it look like if we are effective in achieving a goal? Thus, questions of a theological nature are ignored when congregational goals are put into place. When a group asks, What would it look like if we did it? they and others can inquire if the outcome appropriately expresses Christian faith. Then they will know where they are going and they can create a plan to get there. They can evaluate progress along the way, and they will know when they have arrived.

Much frustration arises in congregations and work groups when there is no clear picture of a possible outcome. There is in the church a naive romanticism about goals, which suggests that a group does not have to think about where it is going or how it is going to get there. Members are asked to "Win souls for Christ." "Increase our evangelistic efforts." "Bring the spirit back into worship." These are not goals. They are pious statements that may have excellent intentions behind them, but each of them will require a description of what the outcome should look like if the group is to be effective. Then a group may ask, Is this really what we meant? Do we know how to achieve the goal? Do we have the resources? Too many groups work on goals with little notion of the end toward which they are working, and then apathy and frustration set in.

Even when leadership groups desire to evaluate, they cannot do so if a group does not know where it is going or how it is going to get there. A prerequisite for evaluation is a description of what would be present if the group has successfully achieved its goal. Leaders can care for committees by assisting them to develop descriptions of what their goal will look like if it is achieved. By doing so, they enhance the ministry and mission of a church and create a healthy environment in which a congregation can adequately evaluate its work.

Part IV

Conclusion

14

Affirming Congregational Life

This book looks at how congregations can be activated; it offers a theory and practice for identifying, focusing, and mobilizing commitments, interests, values, and intentions of members. In the ordinary congregation only a few leaders, including clergy, are active. Most members are passive and inactive. Consequently, congregations are weak and unable to respond well to the challenges of Christian faith, on the one hand, and to the communities in which they live, on the other. Member commitments remain unknown or dormant.

It is no accident when a congregation is inactive. Church tradition and theology have affirmed individualistic activities for the clergy and the ruling elite. Much of contemporary theology points to God's transcendence over individual behavior as, for example, when individuals are saved. The faithful congregation is seldom affirmed as a whole.

In recent years liturgy has been increasingly referred to as celebration. But, again, the emphasis is on the individual celebrating—experiencing ecstasy through tossing balloons, engaging in individual charismatic acts, and singing hymns that dwell on individual feelings. The focus has been on individuals, not on the life of the congregation in worship. Much of contemporary celebration is sterile simply because it is not linked to the experiences of the congregation in ministry and mission. It does not lift up the results of the congregation's commitment and intent. The relationship between experience and statements of faith is lost. When this happens, the symbols and corporate statements of faith lose their power because they have no referents.

The beginning of activation is in the affirmation of congregational life. Each new movement looks back at where the congregation has been in its experience and then makes connections between its experiences of faithfulness and its mission statements, confessions, and tradition. The linking of Christian faith symbols to the common, public life of the congregation makes affirmation possible in two ways. First, when the symbol and experience fit there is cause for thanksgiving and joy that the people have engaged in faithful activity. The symbols are authentic, they point to something concrete in human life. The meaning of Christian faith is affirmed in experience.

Second, when there is discrepancy between symbol and experience, there is cause for confession and the seeking of God's forgiveness. The congregation's confession of sin is based on its experience of its own life of faithlessness. Christian symbols point positively toward congruency between symbol and life, and negatively toward human sin, which in Greek means "missing the mark."

An activated congregation that establishes directions for itself and then engages in self-evaluation affirms both the positive and negative aspects of its life. It offers thanksgiving to God and is joyful in both its congruency and incongruency, because it can affirm God's forgiveness, even in the midst of sinfulness.

Public, common confession makes sense and is appropriate when the public acknowledges that it has sinned. The public life advocated in this book creates the possibility for acknowledging and dealing with all kinds of human error. Affirming communal life places sin within the context of a people who vary in both their commitments and their intentions. Human sin can be openly accepted as an aspect of congregational life, not merely as a private reality which expresses itself only in hidden, private spheres.

Public affirmation of congregational life exposes both individual and corporate sin. The discrepancy between statements of faith and the life of the congregation can be confessed, and forgiveness sought. The difference between goals established and those attained can be brought to the membership for accountability. The poor quality of congregational life can be evaluated, and a fresh commitment to be the body of Christ can be made. Members will no longer be ignored, forgotten, or misused. The relationship between the congregation and the community can be identified and judged by confessions and statements of faith. For example, when a congregation's confession or statement of faith affirms that God is a reconciling God who calls a people to engage in reconciling work, it is possible to reflect critically on relationships within the church and on the ministry of the congregation in the community. Public discussion of the various interpersonal relationships in light of our Christian symbols, can redirect the life of a congregation, which is a pluralistic community. Public discourse about both symbol and experiences creates the possibility for deep and correct understanding in the midst of differences.

Congregational affirmation of its own life is an experience quite different from that of the annual meeting, where dull reports are read and there is no linkage between experience and Christian faith. Little affirmation takes place when the budget is passed and ministry and mission projects are discussed as simple line items. Announcements in church bulletins or from the pulpit are not adequate ways for a congregation to affirm its life.

Few congregations actually know how and in what form their commitments are expressed. Members do not know what their ministry and mission mean to persons and groups who are their beneficiaries. Members of very small congregations may be able to identify the various forms of ministry and mission, but they are not likely to know what they mean to others.

Consequently, little affirmation can take place. Only limited discourse about the relationship between Christian faith and community life is possible. A congregation cannot hold itself accountable until there is sufficient information and enough shared experience to make possible public discussion of any connections between members' understanding and experience of Christian faith. New commitments and intentions cannot be mobilized when members do not have opportunities for thinking as Christians.

When a whole congregation is activated, clergy and lay leaders are challenged to imagine ways to enable the congregation to affirm corporate life. Several congregations have developed annual fairs with booths and a festive atmosphere in which all church and community groups interpret the ministry and mission of the congregation. Special services of worship are created to show the linkage between the experience and the faith of the congregation.

Other churches have developed a "Commitment to the Future" Sunday in which they meet for the day to listen to evaluative task forces share what they have learned about the ministry and mission of the congregation and attempt to direct thinking and commitments into fresh avenues. All presentations and discussions are in small groups. Charts, graphs, posters, tapes of interviews with appropriate people, audio-visual displays made by members, and reports by groups in the community who have received some expression of ministry are shared in an effort to provide all members of the congregation with the most accurate information. The day is divided into different worship services, interspersed with information sharing and discussion. Affirmation, thanksgiving, supplication, proclamation, and confession are aspects of the liturgy of the day as the church community looks to the future.

Leaders of congregations will lead better as they equip congregations to become more Christian. This will happen when they intentionally seek ways to establish congruency between symbols of faith and the life of their congregation. This book describes a theory of activation and activating processes that are offered to leaders as aids to increase the effectiveness of their ministry. Through these processes we can begin to see dry bones come to life.

Appendix

Strategies for Information Gathering and Goal Setting

Additional Ways of Gathering Information

The method of gathering information should be appropriate to the congregation. Smaller congregations in which a high percentage of members attend worship may find a congregational meeting most appropriate for this. Larger congregations may need a variety of ways of gathering information so that all their members can be interviewed. For example, a congregational meeting may be most appropriate for some older members and handicapped people who find it difficult to attend night meetings.

A *congregational meeting* may take place during the hour for a regular worship service. Begin with a brief liturgy, then divide into small groups to share information. End the meeting with prayers and hymns of thanksgiving and supplication for the congregation and community. Another option is a special congregational meeting Sunday afternoon or evening. Divide into small groups and end with a brief service of dedication. Serve dessert.

Task group members may conduct *information gathering sessions in homes of leaders* as a way of enabling members to enter into informal conversation. Participants may be selected geographically. This method will increase the sensitivity to the variety of needs, hopes, concerns, and faith commitments of the congregation. (See Agenda for Home Meetings.)

Gather information from all current groups in the congregation. There are several weaknesses to this method. Information is received from the most active members only and this tends to reflect the implicit and explicit goals already established by the current groups. Members do not hear the hopes and concerns of those not in their groups. New mixes of people offer the possibility of increasing sensitivity and responsiveness to the more complex goals.

Agenda for Home Meetings

Many governing boards have used the homes of active or inactive members for interviewing six to twelve persons living in geographic proximity to one another. Conducting the interviews in the homes of inactive members ensures that these people will be heard and that they will hear what the active members think. The following agenda suggests the length of the meeting, the general style, and the format of the interview. Each governing board should develop its own questions in light of special conditions facing the congregation. The questions should elicit candor about future directions of the congregation.

A. Introductions: 10–17 minutes
    1. Divide into pairs, so that each person may interview another who is not a close friend. Ask the pairs to discover three interesting facts about each other in the time allotted. (2 minutes)
    2. Each person introduces her or his partner to the total group, sharing interesting facts. (15 minutes)
B. Leader might share the purpose of the meeting—to gather information from the congregation in order that congregational goals may be established; to discover what members like about the congregation, what they are concerned about, and what they would be most interested in doing; to discover what less active members of the congregation think about the congregation, its ministry, and its involvement in the community. (3–5 minutes)
C. Gather information. Responses to the following questions should be written on newsprint for all members of the group to see. (60 minutes)
    1. What do you like most about the ministry and mission of the congregation? (10 minutes)
    2. What additional hopes do you have for the life of our church? What needs to happen that is not happening now? (10 minutes)
    3. What specific changes would you like to see in our church? (10 minutes)
    4. In what specific ways do you think the congregation should be ministering to the community? (10 minutes)
    5. Group leaders will summarize and record for the group the most important ideas, facts, and/or feelings which have been shared. (10 minutes)
    6. Circulate a paper among people attending the meeting so that they can indicate their future involvement in the congregation. (A possible format is shown below.) (10 minutes)

Please identify the area of congregational life or of the congregation's ministry to the community in which you are willing to be involved. Please note your hopes and concerns about the congregation as you identify the area where you will be active. In addition, note the number of hours each month you have available for activity in the identified area. (Write your name, address, and telephone number opposite the area you have identified.)

Special Problems in Gathering Information

The following problems in gathering information need to be considered by leaders, and ways to deal with these problems should be discussed in the training session. Interviewers may role play such situations and identify ways these problems can be handled, or the interviewers can discuss possible ways to deal with problems in small groups.

—The leader could be a problem if the group is used as a forum for his or her own ideas and concerns. The principle task is to facilitate—not dominate—the work of the small group.

—A small group may want to focus only on "gripes." Have members clarify the essential idea and move on to other items. Also, the leader can ask for suggestions for action or programs responsive to the expressed concerns.

—Domineering people tend to talk too much and not allow others to contribute. Be sensitive to such a problem and help others to get in. Suggest a process whereby all can contribute their ideas.

—Reticent persons may not think their ideas are important. Help them get their ideas out. A process of moving from person to person will automatically include such people.

—A group may lack faith in the goal-setting process, thinking, It won't make any difference. Assure them that the governing board is prepared to receive all suggestions and will encourage the congregation to work on them.

—A small group may want to reach consensus on the information to be submitted. This is not necessary. Encourage the members to record all data, indicating the most important items.

—Information may be lost or written illegibly. Appoint a reliable scribe to record on newsprint the information and the suggested goal statements.

—A group may suggest unrealistic goals. Test them by asking, Would you be willing to serve on a group that is given this goal and seriously expect to carry it out?

Steps in Goal and Objective Formation

The following process has been developed to provide groups with a systematic, uniform way of setting goals and objectives. Note the places where group discussion and reflection time are needed. These are points where quality thinking by Christians is necessary. Values and commitments are being developed.

The task group and small-group leaders (if additional people have been recruited and trained for home or small-group congregational meetings) should meet together, and the chairperson of the task group should ask the members to answer the following questions:

A. Individual Responses
    1. As I think about what was said in the small group I led, what were seen as the most important areas of congregational life to be included in the goals?
    2. What areas of community life were people most concerned about in the group?
    3. If the congregation does nothing else from this process, what four or five areas seem most important to the group you led? (This should give the larger group a sense of the priorities that may develop.)
B. Group Responses
    1. In teams of two, compare the above responses from leaders of groups with the written information provided from other groups. This process should be organized so that each team reads the newsprint from groups other than its own. Add to the responses given above. Make notes about items for later group discussion. Have the team reflect on priority goals of the congregation suggested by the data.
    2. In plenary session, compare and contrast your lists. Develop a common list of goal areas. This list should reflect an order of priority that the group thinks reflects the information from the small groups. These goal areas should be large and inclusive. For example:
    Goal: To develop a more effective ministry with elderly persons in the community.
    Some objectives:
        (1) By June 30, design and implement a meals-on-wheels program for older persons in the community.
        (2) By October 15, develop a telephone ministry whereby each older person requesting this service will receive two telephone calls daily from a member of the congregation.
        (3) By November 15, purchase a mini-bus and develop a transportation ministry for older people.

The raw data from groups will contain suggestions for both the more inclusive directions and for numerous specific steps. The illustration suggests a broad direction that might be found in the data, and the three objectives are written from suggestions from the data on newsprint.

Reflecting as Christians About Congregational Goals

Most governing boards do not engage in reflection about the quality and nature of congregational life and goals. They may instead use the occasion of implementation of an activating process—such as the one outlined in this book—to do their own reflection and share that with the congregation. Three ways in which a governing board may engage the congregation in such reflection and discussion are described.

1. As the task group gathers information from the congregation and formulates goals and objectives, the governing board can develop a series of criteria designed to characterize the goals and life of the congregation. Examples:

a. A goal of this congregation will be to minister to those in the larger community who have special needs, since this congregation is called to be an agent of God's reconciliation of the world to God.

b. A goal of this congregation will be to minister effectively to members of this congregation who have special needs, since we are called to be members of one body whose different parts share their gifts and resources with one another for the health and vitality of the whole body.

With such a series of statements, the governing board can examine the goals and objectives formulated by the task group and reach conclusions. The outcome could be a statement of its observations in light of the criteria it has developed, recommendations to the congregation in light of its observations, and a list of priorities among the goals in light of its reflections.

The statement of goals and objectives from the task group and the statement of the governing board should be submitted to the congregation at a special meeting called to act on the governing board's report. Groups of six to ten persons should each meet with a member of the governing board and a member of the task group to discuss the two statements and formulate any judgments or recommendations. Members should also be requested at this meeting to volunteer to work on a priority goal and/or objective if they have not previously done so.

2. The governing board appoints a committee whose membership represents the theological diversity of the congregation. These people should have the ability to reflect on the emerging congregational goals that have been formulated by a task group of the governing board. They should provide a theological perspective—a statement of Christian values—on the goals and objectives, which may be presented as a preamble at the time of adoption. They should also develop a critique of the goals and objectives, along with recommendations to the congregation.

The task of this committee is to reflect on the adequacy of the goals and objectives as an expression and interpretation of Christian faith for the congregation and community. They may ask: Is this what we really want to say about ourselves? Is this who we are called by God to be in this community? Is this what we want our actions to say about Christian faith as we implement these goals and objectives? Do we need to challenge the congregation to examine the goals and objectives further because they are trivial, self-centered, only survival oriented, and ignore the needs of the congregation and community?

3. A new organizational design may provide for the appointment of a committee to examine the goals and objectives of the congregation as they are being implemented during the first year. The task is to reflect on the adequacy of the goals and objectives for the congregation in the same manner as the committee described above. This method is important because the full significance of statements often does not appear until there is implementation. Statements that appear trivial or shallow on paper may have great depth when applied.

For Further Reading

This brief bibliography is provided to assist the reader in exploring the texts that lie behind this book. Ideas, assumptions, conceptual framework, and strategies of changing can be found. In developing this bibliography four areas have been included: leadership and transforming activity, theories of transformation or changing, organizational theory and changing, and theological resources that inform and guide transforming ministry. This list is not exhaustive, but it does include the major sources that have informed the understanding of ministry represented in this book.

Adams, John D. *Transforming Work*. Alexandria, Va: Miles River Press, 1984.

Bennis, Warren G., Kenneth D. Benne, and Robert Chin. *The Planning of Change*. New York: Holt, Rinehart, & Winston, 1969.

Brueggemann, Walter. *The Prophetic Imagination*. Philadelphia: Fortress Press, 1978.

Burns, James MacGregor. *Leadership*. New York: Harper & Row, 1978.

Etzioni, Amitai. *The Active Society*. New York: Free Press (Div. of Macmillan Publishing Co.), 1968.

Gamson, William A. *Power and Discontent*. Homewood, Ill.: Dorsey Press, 1968.

Gouldner, Alvin. *The Coming Crisis of Western Sociology*. New York: Basic Books, 1970.

Hall, Brian P. *The Development of Consciousness*. Ramsey, N.J.: Paulist/Newman Press, 1976.

Haroutunian, Joseph. *God With Us*. 2d ed. Allison Park, Pa.: Pickwick Publications, 1991.

Hawkins, Thomas R. *Building God's People*. Nashville, Tennessee: Discipleship Resources, 1990.

Hersey, Paul, and Kenneth H. Blanchard. *Management of Organizational Behavior*. Englewood Cliffs, N.J.: Prentice-Hall, 1977.

Hickman, Craig R., and Michael A. Silva. *Creating Excellence: Managing Corporate Culture, Strategy and Change in the New Age*. New York: New American Library, 1984.

Kanter, Rosabeth Moss. *Men and Women of the Corporation*. New York: Basic Books, 1977.

Koenig, John. *New Testament Hospitality*. Philadelphia: Fortress Press, 1985.

Kouzes, James, and Barry Posner. *The Leadership Challenge*. San Francisco: Jossey-Bass, 1987.

Küng, Hans. *The Church*. Garden City, N.J.: Doubleday & Co., 1967.

———. *Truthfulness*. New York: Sheed and Ward, 1968.

Lippitt, Ronald, Jeanne Watson, and Bruce Westley. *The Dynamics of Planned Change*. New York: Harcourt, Brace & Co., 1958.

Manz, Charles C., and Henry P. Sims. *Super Leadership*. New York: Berkeley Books, 1990.

Niebuhr, H. Richard. *Christ and Culture*. New York: Harper & Brothers, 1951.

Palmer, Parker J. *The Company of Strangers*. New York: Crossroad, 1981.

Perrow, Charles. *Complex Organizations*. New York: Random House, 1979.

———. *Organizational Analysis: A Sociological View*. Belmont, Ca.: Brooks/Cole Publishing Company, 1970.

Ponsioen, J. A. *The Analysis of Social Change Reconsidered*. The Hague, Netherlands: Mouton Publishers, 1965.

Quinn, Robert E., and Kim S. Cameron. *Paradox and Transformation*. Cambridge, Mass.: Ballinger Publishing Co., 1988.

Russell, Letty M. *Household of Freedom*. Louisville: Westminster/John Knox Press, 1987.

Sakenfeld, Katherine Doob. *Faithfulness in Action*. Philadelphia: Fortress Press, 1985.

Sampley, J. Paul. *Pauline Partnership in Christ*. Philadelphia: Fortress Press, 1980.

Schein, Edgar H. *Process Consultation: Its Role in Organizational Development*. Reading, Mass.: Addison-Wesley, 1969.

Tannenbaum, Robert, Margulies Newton, and Fred Massarik. *Human Systems Development*. San Francisco: Jossey-Bass, 1985.

Tichy, Noel M., and Mary Anne Devanna. *The Transformational Leader*. New York: John Wiley & Sons, 1986.

Weiss, Joseph W. *The Management of Change*. New York: Praeger Publishers, 1986.

Wilkins, Alan L. *Developing Corporate Character*. San Francisco: Jossey-Bass, 1989.

Worley, Robert C. *A Gathering of Strangers*. Philadelphia: Westminster Press, 1983.

Zaleznik, Abraham. *The Managerial Mystique*. New York: Harper & Row, 1989.

Index